SRA
Reading Mastery
Signature Edition

Teacher's Guide
Grade 1

Siegfried Engelmann
Elaine C. Bruner

McGraw Hill   SRA

Columbus, OH

READING MASTERY® is a registered trademark of The McGraw-Hill Companies, Inc.

SRAonline.com

 SRA

Send all inquiries to this address:
SRA/McGraw-Hill
4400 Easton Commons
Columbus, OH 43219

Printed in the United States of America.

ISBN: 978-0-07-612465-7
MHID: 0-07-612465-7

12 13 14 15 RMN 15 14 13 12

The **McGraw·Hill** Companies

▪▪▪▪▪▪▪▪▪▪ Contents ▪▪▪▪▪▪▪▪▪

The Grade 1 Program

Children are not to begin the first grade level until they have completed the entire Kindergarten level. Administer the placement test on page 2 for the grade 1 program. Children who do not pass the test should be placed in the Kindergarten level and taught the remainder of the Kindergarten level. Use the Kindergarten mastery tests to determine appropriate placement for children.

INTRODUCTION ■

Reading Mastery, Grade 1 is the second level in the *Reading Mastery Signature Edition* program. The skills, vocabulary, procedures, and instructional details that are presented at the beginning of *Reading Mastery,* Grade 1 are carefully geared to what children learned in *Reading Mastery,* Grade K. The *Reading Mastery* program controls all aspects of reading development through the direct teaching of every skill needed for decoding and comprehension. Extensive practice reinforces all skills and strategies.

PROGRAM MATERIALS

The following materials are for the teacher's use. They are included in the *Reading Mastery,* Grade 1 kit.

1. *Three Presentation Books.* These books provide a script for each task in each lesson. They tell the teacher what to say and what to do. They specify correct responses, and they tell the teacher how to correct incorrect responses.

   Planning Pages appear every 20 lessons. These present an overview of the skills taught, a summary of special considerations for upcoming lessons, and additional reading activities.

   • Presentation Book A covers Lessons 1 to 48.
   • Presentation Book B covers Lessons 49 to 104.
   • Presentation Book C covers Lessons 105 to 160.

2. The Workbook *Answer Key.* This book contains reduced copies of the pages from all three student Workbooks. Correct answers are indicated on the pages.

3. *The Spelling Presentation Book.* This book contains instructions for presenting the 160 spelling lessons. Further information about the spelling program is contained in the introduction to the Spelling Presentation Book.

4. *The Teacher's Guide.* The Teacher's Guide, which you are now reading, provides a rationale for each skill taught in *Reading Mastery,* Grade 1 and detailed information on how to teach the program and how to correct when the children make mistakes.

5. *One Skills Profile Folder.* This folder contains a summary of the skills taught in the program and provides a space for indicating when a child has mastered each skill. One folder is needed for each child.

   In addition, there are group progress indicators (various-colored clips, which allow the teacher to mark the last lesson completed by each group), and a transparency (a clear plastic page that can be placed over the pages of the Presentation Books to protect them from smudges).

Each child should have the following:

1. *Two Storybooks.* These books are used by the children. The Storybooks have hard covers and are reusable. (One copy of each book is included in the teacher's kit.)

2. *Three Workbooks.* Each child is to have one set of these books. They contain seatwork activities for each of the 160 lessons in *Reading Mastery,* Grade 1, including story comprehension items, following written directions, writing practice, new reading comprehension items, and picture comprehension. The Workbooks are not reusable.

1. *Independent Readers. Reading Mastery,* Grade 1 has optional Independent Reader Libraries. See Appendix page 103.

2. *Curriculum Based Assessment* and *Fluency Handbook. Reading Mastery,* Grade 1 has an optional and complete system for monitoring student performance.

PLACEMENT

No placement test is required for children who met the final Fluency: Rate/Accuracy criterion in *Reading Mastery,* Grade K. Place those children as follows:

- Children who passed all individual Fluency Checkouts on their first attempt (without first failing a checkout and then later making it up) start at lesson 11 of *Reading Mastery,* Grade 1 and proceed at the rate of one lesson a day.
- Children who initially failed some individual Fluency Checkouts but who successfully passed the final Fluency Checkout at lesson 160 start at lesson 1 in *Reading Mastery,* Grade 1 and proceed at the rate of one lesson a day.

The placement test should be presented to the following children:

- Children who completed more than 135 lessons of *Reading Mastery,* Grade K, but who did not complete all 160 lessons. (Children who did not get as far as lesson 135 in *Reading Mastery,* Grade K are to continue where they left off at the end of the year and are to complete *Reading Mastery,* Grade K before starting *Reading Mastery,* Grade 1.)
- Children who initially failed the final Fluency Checkout at lesson 160 of *Reading Mastery,* Grade K.
- Children who are to be placed in a *Reading Mastery* program after completing one year of instruction in another reading program.

Placement Test

The test appears on page 1 of *Storybook 1.* A copy appears below, with the instructions for administering the test.

Present the placement test to each child individually before beginning *Reading Mastery,* Grade 1. Children are not to observe other children taking the placement test before they take the test themselves.

Instructions: I want you to read this story very carefully. Take your time. Start with the title and read the story as well as you can.

---

the cow on the rōad

lots of men went down the rōad in a littlₑ car.

a cow was sitting on the rōad. sō the men ran to the cow. "wē will lift this cow," they said.

but the men did not lift the cow. "this cow is sō fat wē can not lift it."

the cow said, "I am not sō fat. I can lift mē." then the cow got in the car.

the men said, "now wē can not get in the car." sō the men sat on the rōad and the cow went hōmₑ in the car.

the end

Story 1 Placement Test

102 words/**2.5 min** = 41 wpm

Allow each child 2½ minutes to read the passage. Stop the child who hasn't finished after 2½ minutes. Record each child's time and tally the child's errors on a test summary form. A sample appears here.

Placement Test Summary Form

Child's Name	Number of Errors	Time (min:sec)	Entry Lesson	Instructional Group
Joel	7	2:19		
Maria	2	1:46		
Sandy	13	2:30		

Count any of the following as errors:

1. If a child misidentifies a word, tell the child the word and mark an error.

2. If a child "self-corrects," saying the word incorrectly and then identifying it correctly, mark an error.

3. If a child fails to identify a word after about four seconds, tell the child the word and mark an error.

4. If a child omits a word, point to the place where the word was omitted. If the child correctly reads the word, do not record an error.

5. If a child skips a line of text, point to the appropriate line. If the child correctly reads the words, do not record an error.

6. For the first word a child sounds out instead of saying it fast, (*wwweeennnt* instead of *went*), ask, "What word is that?" If the child identifies the word, do not record an error. If the child sounds it out again, record an error. After the first word a child sounds out, do not ask, "What word is that?" Mark one error for each word that is sounded out.

7. If a child repeats a word or words more than twice in a sentence, mark an error.

8. If a child does not finish the passage during the 2½ minute timing, count every word *not* read as an error.

Placing the Children in the Program

1. Children who score no more than 3 errors on the entire story begin with lesson 11 and do one lesson a day, except as specified in the Presentation Book.

2. Children who score between 4 and 8 errors begin at lesson 1 and do one lesson a day, except as specified in the Presentation Book.

3. Children who make more than 8 errors are placed in *Reading Mastery,* Grade K. To determine an appropriate placement for these children, give them the individual Fluency Checkouts from *Reading Mastery,* Grade K, Presentation Book C and the Storybooks. Start with the Fluency Checkout for lesson 140. If a child passes this Fluency Checkout, place the child at lesson 141. If a child does not pass it, present the Fluency Checkout for lesson 130. Continue in this manner until the child passes a Fluency Checkout. Place the child in the lesson number following the Fluency Checkout that the child passes.

Here is a sample test summary form indicating the group and lesson placement for each child.

Placement Test Summary Form

Child's Name	Number of Errors	Time (min:sec)	Entry Lesson	Instructional Group
Joel	7	2:19	1	b
Maria	2	1:46	11	a
Sandy	13	2:30	121 (RM)	c

Initial Grouping of the Children

Here are the rules for initially grouping the children:

1. If possible, avoid dividing the class into more than three small groups.

2. Make the lowest-performing group the smallest, preferably with no more than five or six children.

3. Make the higher-performing groups larger. The top group and the middle group may contain as many as twelve children.

4. As the children progress through the program, the groups may be made larger.

In-Program Tests

Reading Mastery, Grade 1 contains three types of in-program tests: Reading Hard Words; Reading Accuracy Tests; and Individual Fluency Checkouts: Rate/Accuracy. All the tests appear in your Presentation Books at the lesson in which they are to be given. Each test contains

   (a) directions for administering and scoring and
   (b) procedures for reteaching skills, skipping lessons, or readministering the test.

A list of the in-program tests appears below. Note that, from lesson 40 until the end of the program (lesson 160), the only type of test presented is the individual Fluency Checkout. It occurs in every fifth lesson in the program.

Presentation Book A

Lesson 4	Reading **hard words** in reader test
Lesson 5	Individual **Fluency Checkout**
Lesson 9	Reading **hard words** in reader test
Lesson 10	Individual **Fluency Checkout**
Lesson 13	Reading **hard words** in reader test
Lesson 15	Individual **Fluency Checkout**
Lesson 20	Group **reading accuracy** test and Individual **Fluency Checkout**
Lesson 25	Individual **Fluency Checkout**
Lesson 26	Group **reading accuracy** test
Lesson 30	Individual **Fluency Checkout**
Lesson 35	Individual **Fluency Checkout**
Lesson 36	Group **reading accuracy** test
Lesson 40	Individual **Fluency Checkout**
Lesson 45	Individual **Fluency Checkout**

Presentation Books B and C

Lesson 50	Individual **Fluency Checkout**
Lessons 55 to 160	(Every 5 lessons) **Individual Fluency: Rate/ Accuracy Checkout**

Reading Hard Words

Lessons that present a reading-hard-words exercise have no story and no additional reading-vocabulary exercises. In the reading-hard-words exercise, the children individually read a column of words. Reading-hard-words exercises occur in lessons 3, 4, 8, 9, 13, 18, 32, and 47. In the test version (lessons 4, 9, and 13), a scoring key tells the teacher whether to firm the children or to proceed to the next lesson in the program. (See page 23 for firming procedures.)

Below are the teacher and student materials for the reading-hard-words exercise that appears in lesson 13. Step *f* is the test scoring key.

READING HARD WORDS 13

Exercise 4 is a test of reading accuracy. Tally all reading errors on a separate sheet.

EXERCISE 4

Hard words in reader

You'll present rewards in this exercise.

a. You're going to read hard words today. Keep your reader open to page 21. ✔

b. If you can read all of the words in a column without making a mistake, you'll get ____. (Reward the children with stars, points, etc.)

c. (Call on a child.) Read the words in the first column. Start at the top and go down the column. Everybody, touch the words that are being read. Raise your hand if you hear a mistake.

d. (Call on another child to read the second column.)

e. (Give each child a turn at reading one column of words. Praise the children who read each word in the column without making a mistake. Children who make a mistake must repeat the word until firm.)

To Correct

1. (Immediately say the correct word.)
2. (Tell the child who made the mistake:) Touch that word. (Pause.) What word?
3. (Then tell the child:) Now go back to the top of the column and read the words again.

f. (If the children average more than one mistake, do not proceed to lesson 14. See the Teacher's Guide for details.)

Lesson 13 Presentation Book

---

līked	barking	when
swim	that	there
fōr	hēre	other
get	shē	funny
got	they	hōrse
end	where	cāme
and	how	give
at	whȳ	trying
āte	dōn't	rīding
ēat	didn't	hard

Lesson 13 Storybook

Individual Fluency Checkouts: Rate/Accuracy

The individual checkout for Fluency: Rate/Accuracy occurs as the last exercise of the lesson. The Fluency Checkouts occur every five lessons beginning at lesson 5. During a Fluency Checkout, the children individually read a passage from their Storybook to the teacher. Shown below is the first individual Fluency Checkout.

★ **INDIVIDUAL CHECKOUT**
EXERCISE 19

2½-minute individual fluency checkout: rate/accuracy

(Make a permanent chart with children's names and lesson numbers. See the Teacher's Guide for a sample chart.)

a. As you are doing your worksheet, I'll call on children one at a time to read the **whole story**. If you can read the whole story in less than two and a half minutes, and if you make no more than three errors, I'll put two stars after your name on the chart for lesson 5.

b. If you make too many errors or don't read in less than two and a half minutes, you'll have to practice and do it again. When you do read it in under two and a half minutes with no more than three errors, you'll get one star. Remember, two stars if you can do it the first time, one star if you do it the second or third time you try.

c. (Call on each child. Tell the child:) Start with the title and read the whole story carefully. Go. (Time the child. If the child makes a mistake, quickly tell the child the correct word and permit the child to continue reading. As soon as the child makes the fourth error or exceeds the time limit, tell the child to stop.) You'll have to read the story to yourself and try again later. (Plan to monitor the child's practice.)

d. (Record two stars for each child who reads appropriately. Congratulate those children.)

e. (Give children who do not earn two stars a chance to read the story again before the next lesson is presented. Award one star to each of those children who meet the rate and accuracy criterion.)
113 words/**2.5 min** = 45 wpm **[3 errors]**

Lesson 5

An individual Fluency Checkout Chart appears on page 111 of this guide. The chart may be reproduced for use in your classroom.

Reading Accuracy Tests

The reading accuracy tests are presented as part of the story reading for specified lessons. The teacher tallies all first-reading errors (whether they are made by the group or by individual children). The performance criteria for each test appear in the presentation materials for the lesson. These criteria indicate whether the children are to repeat lessons, proceed to the next lesson, or skip specified lessons. The criteria from lesson 20 are shown below.

★ **GROUP ACCURACY TEST**

Place the group on the basis of story reading accuracy for the first reading of story 20.

1. If the group scored between 5 and 8 errors, proceed to lesson 21 as the next reading lesson.

2. If the group scored less than 5 errors, skip lessons 21 and 22 and present lesson 23 as the next reading lesson.

3. If the group scored more than 8 errors, repeat lesson 19 as the next reading lesson. On the following day present lesson 20. The test for reading accuracy in lesson 20 is to be repeated as part of lesson 20.

Lesson 20

Skipping

Reading Mastery, Grade 1 is designed so that faster groups can complete the 160 lessons in 143 school days. To achieve the maximum number of skips, the group would enter at lesson 11 (not at lesson 1) on the basis of placement-test performance. The group would then meet the skipping criteria for each of the three reading accuracy tests. This performance would allow them to skip an additional seven lessons.

Regrouping Children

The in-program tests have these purposes:

1. They make sure that children are firm on critical skills before they proceed in the program.
2. They give you feedback about your presentations—to let you know if you are actually firming the children when you present lessons, or if you are not repeating examples enough to make sure the children know exactly what to do.
3. They give you information about children who do not belong in a particular small group.

The information about the children's performance is particularly important for regrouping the children. The placement test gives you information about how each child performs at the beginning of the year, but it does not tell you how fast the child will progress. Some children start with fewer skills and progress rapidly. Others start with more skills but proceed more slowly.

Plan to regroup the children several times during the year. Here are the steps to follow for identifying the children who should be placed in another group:

1. A child who passes nearly every test and who performs well in the group should be considered for placement in a higher group.
2. A child who passes most of the tests is appropriately grouped.
3. A child who continually fails tests should be considered for placement in a lower-performing group.
4. A child who continually fails tests and who is in the bottom group should receive additional help on critical skills.

SCHEDULING THE DAILY READING LESSONS

Schedule reading for the same time each day.
- Allow thirty minutes for teacher-directed work with each reading group.
- Allow another fifteen to twenty minutes each day for the children to work independently at their desks on the Worksheet activities.
- Allow twenty minutes each day to check the independent work of the children and to remedy problems. Note that you are not merely to mark papers and hand them back to the children. If a child makes an error, you are to diagnose the problem and actually correct the source of the error by firming the weak skill.

- Allow ten minutes for each spelling lesson from the *Reading Mastery,* Grade 1 spelling program (Lessons 1–160). Spelling can be presented to the entire class or to small groups. Spelling is not presented as part of the reading lesson.

Here is a sample schedule:

Time	Group A	Group B	Group C
9:00–9:30	Teacher works with this group.	These groups do work in reading and other independent work.	
9:30–10:00	This group does work in reading and other independent work.	Teacher works with this group.	This group does work in reading and other independent work.
10:00–10:30	These groups do work in reading and other independent work.		Teacher works with this group.
10 minutes daily for each spelling lesson	The spelling lessons can be presented to either the entire class or to small groups.		

USING THE PRESENTATION BOOKS

The three Presentation Books, books A, B, and C, provide the teacher with directions for presenting each task and also provide display material—the symbols and words—to be shown to the children.

The Presentation Books are divided into lessons. The number of the lesson appears at the top and bottom of every page. The first page of the lesson is indicated by the word *Lesson* preceding the number: the last page of the lesson is indicated by the words *End of Lesson* followed by the number of the lesson.

In each lesson the exercise headings, such as *Sounds, Reading Vocabulary,* or *Story,* indicate the major skills to be developed in the exercises that follow. Track headings are printed in boldface

capitals. If a track has not been presented before, its title is preceded by a red star ★.

The exercises that you present are numbered, and the number of each exercise is followed by a brief description of that exercise's objectives.

Here are the exercise conventions:
- What you are to **<u>say</u>** is in blue type.
- (What you are to <u>do</u> is in black type.)
- *The spoken responses expected from the children are in italics.*
- As you progress through the lessons, you will notice that there are black lines above and below some of the exercise headings. The rules signal the introduction of a new format. A new exercise format presents a significant change in the method of presenting a exercise.

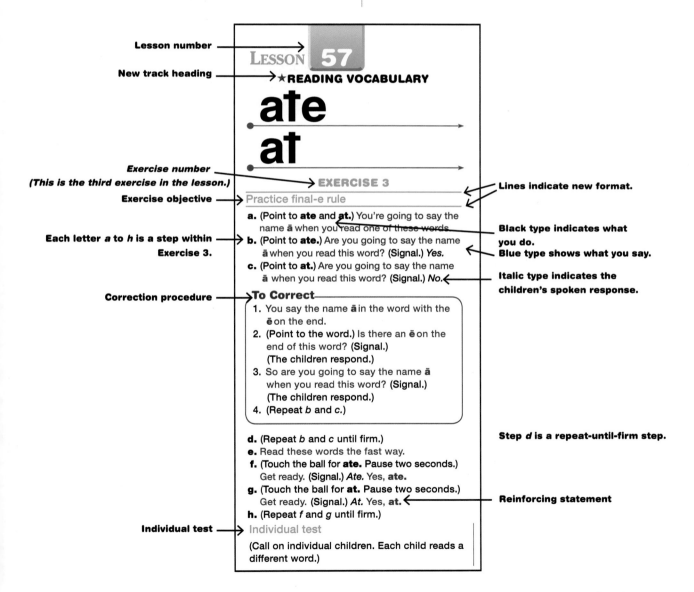

The daily lesson is divided into three parts:
- In the first part, the teacher presents exercises from the Presentation Book to the children in the group. For most of these exercises, the display material is contained in the Presentation Book and is shown to the children.
- In the second part, the children read from their Storybooks. The Presentation Book provides the teacher with specific exercises that are to be presented as the children read the story. The Presentation Book also provides the teacher with the details on how to direct the reading of the story.
- In the third part of the lesson, the children work on their Worksheet activities for the lesson. The Worksheet for a given lesson consists of one workbook sheet, printed on two sides.

In some lessons, Worksheet activities are teacher-directed, which means that the teacher takes the children through each step in working particular Worksheet activities. In other lessons, the children complete the entire Worksheet independently. Specific directions for the presentation of each Worksheet activity appear in the Presentation Book.

USING THE TEACHER'S GUIDE

The Teacher's Guide is designed to be a reference book that provides specific information on presenting exercises. The guide divides the program into three lesson blocks:
- Block One: Lessons 1–39 (Firming)
- Block Two: Lessons 40–80 (Vowel Mechanics)
- Block Three: Lessons 81–160 (Textbook Preparation)

The blocks provide you with a rough schedule for pre-service and in-service work and for rehearsing new exercises before presenting them to the children. The guide contains information about how to present each new major skill taught in the various blocks.

Before starting the program, master all the practice exercises that are specified for Block One. Block One contains basic training information and exercises that should be presented as part of a basic pre-service and an ongoing in-service program.

When your top group of children reaches lesson 20, begin practicing the exercises specified in Block Two. And when your top group reaches lesson 60, start practicing the exercises that appear in Block Three.

Consult the Teacher's Guide if your children are having trouble with specific exercises. The Teacher's Guide provides great detail on how to present and how to correct. Most major formats are discussed with emphasis on critical behaviors and specific corrections that may be required at different parts of the exercises.

TEACHING STRATEGIES

How to Set Up the Group

1. Seat the children in a semicircle in front of you. Sit so that you can observe every child in the group, as well as the children who are engaged in independent work. Children in the group should sit on chairs, not at desks.

2. Test to see that all children can see the Presentation Book. Do this by holding your head next to the book and looking to see whether you can see the eyes of all the children. If you have to look almost sideways from the book to see a child's eyes, that child won't be able to see what is on the page.

3. Keep all the children within touching distance. There will be times during the lesson when you will want to hand the Presentation Book to a child, or to touch the children to reinforce them. This will be easier if the children are all within arm's reach of you. Sit close to the children and group them close together.

4. Place the lowest performers directly in front of you, in the first row if there is more than one row. Seat the highest performers on the ends of the group, or in the second row. You will naturally look most frequently at the children seated directly in front of you. You want to teach until every child is firm. If you are constantly looking at the lowest-performing children, you will know when they are firm. When the lowest-performing children are firm, the rest of the group will be firm.

Getting into the Lesson

1. On the first day that you begin a lesson, introduce the rules that the group is to follow. Tell the children what they are expected to do. Summarize the rules: "Sit tall, look at the book, and talk big." Note that these rules express precisely what the children are supposed to do. Reinforce them for following the rules.

2. Get into the lesson *quickly.* If the group is shy or tends to present behavior problems, begin by telling the children "Stand up . . . touch your nose . . ." until all of them are responding without hesitation. This activity gets the children responding and establishes you as directing what they are to do. Then quickly present the first exercise.

3. Present each exercise until the children are firm. The best time to get them all responding together until firm is the first time an exercise is presented. This establishes your criterion of performance. Further information on teaching to criterion appears below.

4. Use clear signals. All signals have the same purpose—to trigger a simultaneous response from the group. All signals have the same rationale—if you can get the group to respond simultaneously, with no child leading the others, you will get information about the performance of all the children, not just those who happen to answer first. The only alternative that gives you as much information about the children is to give each child an individual turn on each exercise, a procedure that takes a great deal of time and usually promotes behavior problems among those children who are waiting for their turns.

5. Pace exercises appropriately. Pacing is the rate at which different parts of an exercise are presented. Not all portions of an exercise should be presented at the same rate.

   Different pacing is specified throughout the guide. Many of the formats contain such instructions as "pause one second," or "pause three seconds."

   Note that all signals are paced with the same timing. The children learn that the signal will follow one second after you stop talking in an exercise. Keep this interval constant.

6. Reinforce the children's good performance. Make your praise specific. If the children are working hard on a difficult skill, tell them so.

Teaching to Criterion

At the conclusion of any exercise, every child should be able to perform the exercise independently, without any need for corrections. Children are "at criterion" or "firm" on an exercise only when they can perform immediately with the correct response. Your goal is to teach so that every child is at criterion.

Let the children know what your criterion is. Keep on an exercise until you can honestly say to them, "Terrific. Everybody read every word correctly." If your criterion is strict for an exercise, your group will have less difficulty with similar exercises in subsequent lessons.

Individual Turns

Individual turns are specified in the exercises or under the heading *Individual Test.* There are several rules to follow when administering individual turns:

1. Present individual turns only after the group is firm. If you go to individual turns too soon, some of the children will not be able to give a firm response. If you wait until the children are firm on group responses, the chances are much better that each will be able to give a firm response on an individual turn.

2. Give most of your individual turns to the lowest-performing children in the group—those children seated directly in front of you. By watching these children during the group practice of an exercise, you can tell when they are ready to perform individually. When the lowest performers can perform the exercise without correction, you can safely assume that the other children in the group are also able to perform the exercise.

3. Some exercises do not specify individual turns. If you are in doubt about the performance of any children on these exercises, present quick individual turns. Always include the individual turns for exercises in which they are specified.

4. The following procedure is recommended for administering individual turns once group responses on a exercise are firm. First, you can state: "Time for individual turns." Then focus on the exercise for students to think and practice. Finally, call on an individual student to respond to the exercise. This procedure helps to keep the entire group alert to you and practicing the exercise until a specific student's name is called.

DEVELOPMENT OF MAJOR TRACKS OR SKILLS

Children who enter the *Reading Mastery,* Grade 1 program should be able to decode words that are presented in the unique *Reading Mastery* orthography.

thē fat man sāiled on a ship.

They should have had practice in handling simple reading-comprehension exercises, including responding to written questions about stories. The children should be able to read a word at a time (without sounding out) and should be fairly proficient at decoding.

The *Reading Mastery,* Grade 1 program builds on these skills. The program teaches new skills for sound-letter analysis, for attacking and analyzing words, for story reading, and for working independently. The scope and sequence chart on page 112 outlines the track development of the program.

SOUNDS, LETTER NAMES, AND ORTHOGRAPHY

At the beginning of *Reading Mastery,* Grade 1, which is compatible with *Reading Mastery,* Grade K, children read a highly prompted orthography, one with joined letters and long lines over long vowels. The orthographic prompts are gradually dropped until, by lesson 86, the children are reading only standard orthography. They continue to read words and stories in standard orthography through the remaining lessons of the program. Below is a summary of how the orthography changes as the program progresses.

Letters Taught as Sounds (Lessons 1–39)

At the beginning of the program, all letters are identified as "sounds." These sounds, which are taught in *Reading Mastery,* Grade K, allow children to read most words by identifying the sounds and joining them together. Included in the symbols for sounds are joined letters (**th, sh, ch, iñg, er, oo, wh, qu**), and letters with long lines over them (**ā, ē, ī, ō, ū**). Forty sounds are taught in *Reading Mastery,* Grade K. They are reviewed in lessons 1 to 39 of *Reading Mastery,*

Grade 1. At the beginning of *Reading Mastery,* Grade 1, all sounds, except *l,* appear as lowercase letters.

Sound Combinations (Lessons 1–45)

The following sound combinations are taught in lessons 1 through 45: *ar,* pronounced "are"; *al,* pronounced "all"; and *ou,* pronounced "ow" as in "out."

A pronunciation guide and list of sounds is on the inside back cover of this Teacher's Guide.

Names of Vowels (Lessons 40–52)

During this lesson range, children are taught letter names for vowels. The long vowels are presented with no lines over them. (The names are the letter sounds that were taught when these letters had long lines over them.)

Disjoining of Previously Joined Letter Combinations (Lessons 67–81)

At lesson 67, *th* is disjoined; at lesson 72, *sh* is disjoined; at lesson 76, *ing* is disjoined. Other joined letters—*wh, ch, oo, qu, er*—are unjoined in reading vocabulary from lesson 81. Sound combinations for the disjoined letters are periodically reviewed through the end of *Reading Mastery,* Grade 1.

Traditional Textbook Print (Lessons 81–160)

Traditional print is first introduced in reading vocabulary (lesson 81), and later in the Storybook (lesson 84) and Workbook (lesson 86). Individual capital letters appear after they have been taught. By lesson 94 all capitals are introduced.

Letter Names (Lessons 83–86)

During this lesson range, letter names for all the lowercase letters are taught.

Capital Letters (Lessons 87–94)

Starting at lesson 87, capital letters are taught by name. Capitals that many children have difficulty identifying (*A, R, D, E, Q, B, L, H, G*) receive extra practice to guarantee learning.

READING VOCABULARY EXERCISES

In every lesson, the children work on reading-vocabulary exercises. These exercises involve lists of words that are not presented in the context of a story or sentence. Following the reading-vocabulary exercises, the children read stories composed of words they have been taught. The reading vocabulary is designed to teach words at a relatively fast rate. By the end of *Reading Mastery*, Grade 1, children have learned nearly 1700 new words.

The reading vocabulary is designed to achieve the following objectives:

1. To firm and reinforce the child's recognition of simple, regularly-spelled words that were introduced in *Reading Mastery*, Grade K: *man, sat, in, went,* and so on.

2. To firm the irregular words presented in *Reading Mastery*, Grade K: *was, said, of, do, walk, talk,* and so on.

3. To introduce an analysis of words that have common sound combinations, such as *al (always), ar (arm), ou (shout), ea (meat),* and *ee (need)*. Note that not all sound combinations are introduced in the Reading Vocabulary track. Although children will be able to read such words as paint and boat, the sound combinations *ai* and *oa* are not introduced.

4. To present an analysis of words that have endings such as *s, ed, ing,* or *er* so that children can appropriately attack these words, even when all letters are full-sized and unjoined. Early in the program, the word *walked* is written this way:

walk**e**d

Later, the *e* becomes full-sized.

5. To teach children to handle words that end in *e* and follow the long-vowel rule *(same, fine, home)*. The analysis of these words is performed when the words are presented with no long line over the vowel and with a full-sized *e* on the end. Early in the program, the word *home* would be written this way:

When the analysis of long-vowel words begins, the word is written this way:

home

6. To teach children the procedure of breaking words into parts, analyzing known parts, and then chaining them together *(yourself, anybody,* and so on).

7. To teach children to attend to the spelling of words.

8. To expand the children's reading vocabulary so they have enough words by the end of *Reading Mastery*, Grade 1 to read material that is written at the third-grade level. Nearly all of the basic words from vocabulary-frequency lists (including contractions) are taught.

The structure of the program ensures that the words, the attack skills, and the conventions are not merely presented to the children—they are taught to the children. In almost every lesson, twenty to thirty words are presented. During the first half of the program, some of these words are sounded out and then identified. Some are read the fast way without sounding out. For some, the teacher covers the last part of the word and has the children read the entire word the fast way.

During the last half of the program, words are read the fast way, and some words are also spelled. Children sometimes identify part of a longer word, then identify the whole word.

A given word appears an average of about five times in the reading vocabulary. Some words appear as many as twenty-five times. The same word will not always be presented the same way. Children may analyze the same word different ways in various lessons—sounding it out, analyzing it as a two-part word, or spelling the word. This approach provides the children with a variety of strategies for attacking words.

STORY READING

Children read 152 stories during the group story-reading part of the lessons. They respond to a wide range of oral comprehension questions presented by the teacher. In addition, they independently read almost two hundred comprehension passages during their independent-workbook-practice time. Children write answers to questions for each story and for each comprehension passage as they work independently.

The stories, written especially for the program, provide high interest for students from many backgrounds, and cumulatively review words and patterns that have been taught. The selections present words and patterns in both a story context and in the context of science and social-studies passages. Stories such as *The Ugly Duckling, The Boy Who Cried "Wolf,"* and *The Lion and the Mouse* are favorites that have been adapted for *Reading Mastery,* Grade 1.

The stories are closely correlated with the reading vocabulary. See the listing of vocabulary words on pages 105–110 of this guide. Early in the program, new words or types of words are presented in reading vocabulary for two to four lessons before these words appear in stories. The lag time between the introduction of words in reading vocabulary and the appearance of the words in the stories is reduced in later lessons. By lesson 45 some words are introduced in the story in the same lesson in which they first appear in the reading vocabulary. This procedure is designed to let the children know that they will use the words that are introduced in the reading vocabulary and that they will be held accountable for identifying these words when they appear in stories.

After the children have been taught how to read long-vowel words with a final *e*, a number of stories are introduced that contain these words and the short-vowel words most easily confused with them. Words such as *hate-hat, cone-con, pin-pine, slop-slope* reinforce the teaching that was provided in the reading-vocabulary exercises.

In summary, by the end of the *Reading Mastery,* Grade 1 program, the children have had a great deal of experience in reading a basic vocabulary of several thousand words. These words include words with the sound combinations *al, ou, ar, ea,* and *ee.* The children read from traditional orthography (with *th, sh, ch, ing, er, oo, wh, qu,* unjoined). All letters are full-sized, and capital letters appear in appropriate places. Children also discriminate words such as *made-mad* and *rod-rode.*

Comprehension

The types of comprehension activities involved in the stories are carefully controlled. In early stories the story line is fairly simple and the sentences are straightforward. Later stories involve more sophisticated information. The last series of stories in the program, for example, involve a girl who dreams that she is in a strange land that is governed by a series of highly improbable rules, such as "Every dusty path leads to the lake." Before the girl can leave this strange land, she must learn all the rules. The children who read this series of fifteen stories must also learn the rules and must apply them to situations that occur in the stories.

Introducing rules and information into the stories ensures that the children become facile in handling the kind of information and operations that are assumed by textbook work.

By the end of the program
- The children have been introduced to a full range of comprehension questions.
- They have learned to draw conclusions from facts presented in their stories.
- They have practiced saying what a character in a story says (quotation saying).
- They have worked with serial stories in which information from one story is reviewed in the next.
- They have handled stories that involve new information and rules that are applied to different situations.

Fluency: Rate/Accuracy

Children are checked on their oral reading every fifth lesson. They read a specified selection from a story to the teacher. Procedures for improving children's reading fluency and accuracy are detailed later in this guide.

Supplementary Reading

The children should be encouraged to supplement their classroom reading with their own independent reading. A listing of available Independent Readers appears on page 103 of this guide. These Independent Readers consist of vocabulary and orthography keyed to specific lesson ranges in the program. This list is followed by an annotated list of suitable outside reading books. You might use these lists to stock your own classroom library or ask your librarian to have the titles available for your students.

THE WORKSHEETS

The Workbooks contain daily worksheets that
- Reinforce reading and related skills that have been taught during the teacher-directed part of the reading lesson
- Provide practice in reading silently and working independently
- Introduce new skills, such as following instructions and making deductions, that are required for future academic work, particularly work related to handling textbook instructions and information
- Give children practice in remembering information that was presented in the stories they read during any previous reading lessons
- Give children some practice in writing.

On a typical worksheet, four to eight activities appear. They always include story items, which are questions about the story that was read on that day or on preceding days. Other worksheet activities include reading comprehension, following instructions, and making deductions.

Each activity is designed so that the items become increasingly difficult or more complex as the lessons progress. The first type of item in each track is quite simple and generally appears until the children are perfectly firm. More difficult items are then systematically introduced.

For example, in the Following-Instructions track, the items from lesson 18 are of this form:

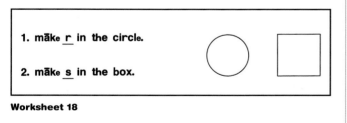

Worksheet 18

A later variation from lesson 31 is of this form:

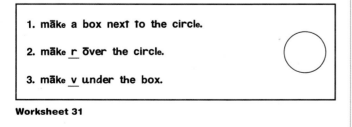

Worksheet 31

Finally, the children work items of this form, from lesson 120:

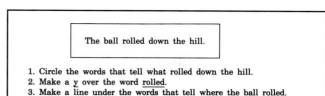

Worksheet 120

When the children have completed all the Work activities, they are familiar with
- Independent paragraph reading
- Answering comprehension items by filling in the blanks, by circling the appropriate choices for the blanks, by making boxes under the answers, and so on
- Answering questions that involve such discriminations as *what, who, when, why, how many,* and *is*
- Referring to a picture and answering questions about what is illustrated
- Handling basic deduction forms such as this item from lesson 133:

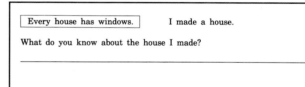

Worksheet 133

- Applying written rules to illustrations, such as the following from lesson 131:

Worksheet 131

The goal of the *Reading Mastery*, Grade 1 program is not merely to teach children better decoding skills. The program contains a broad range of comprehension activities, and the program has provisions for actually teaching these skills, not merely exposing the children to them.

A summary of the various kinds of comprehension activities that are presented in the *Reading Mastery*, Grade 1 program follows.

Comprehension Activities Directed by the Teacher

1. *Stories,* lessons 1–160. Children read in their readers. You ask questions during the first or second reading of the story. The questions are specified in the Presentation Books. Questions that relate to the story picture are presented after the reading of each story.

2. *Read the Item(s),* lessons 3–94. In their readers, children read one-sentence items such as, "When the teacher says 'go', hold up your hands." After the children read the item, you do the action that the item specifies. The children then perform the action specified for them.

Comprehension Activities Performed Independently

1. *Story Items,* lessons 1–160. These are pencil-and-paper tasks in which children read questions about the story they read in the structured group presentation. The questions involve a variety of responses from the children, such as circling the correct answer, writing the answer in the blank, completing the sentence, underlining the answer. In the later part of the program, different story items in the same lesson have individual directions. One item may instruct the children to circle the answer and the next may direct them to write the word in the blank.

2. *Story-Items Review,* lessons 101–147. These are pencil-and-paper tasks that deal with stories that were read in earlier lessons. They require the children to retain information.

3. *Picture Comprehension,* lessons 1–25. These items involve a Worksheet picture and items that ask information about things illustrated in the picture. Children respond by writing in the word that is missing in each sentence that describes the picture.

4. *Story-Picture Items,* lessons 61–94. These items involve pictures that appear in the Storybook. Children read the items, refer to the details of the picture, and write the answers to the items.

5. *Worksheet Reading Comprehension,* lessons 8–160. One or two passages with comprehension items appear on each Worksheet. Children read the passage and respond to the items. The vocabulary, length, and complexity of the passages parallel the presentation of skills that are taught during the structured reading lessons. Many passages in lessons 132 to 160 deal with new information or *Factual Information.*

6. *Following Instructions Type 1,* lessons 18–60. These items involve figures (a circle or a box) and instructions that tell the children how to operate on the figures. Early instructions may involve making *s* over the circle and making *r* in the box. Later instructions involve writing words in the places specified by the instructions.

7. *Following Instructions Type 2,* lessons 47–120. These exercises present a sentence in a box. Below the box are items that direct the children to circle, underline, or make a line over a specified word or words in the sentence.

8. *Picture Deductions,* lessons 95–147. These items present a rule, such as, "If a girl is swimming, she is tall." Six girls are illustrated, some are swimming. The illustrations do not indicate height. The children apply the rule and circle every girl that is tall.

9. *Written Deductions Type 1,* lessons 123–147. These exercises involve a rule, such as, "Every tiger is mean," and items such as "Zag is a tiger. What do you know about Zag?"

10. *Written Deductions Type 2,* lessons 148–160. These exercises are similar to picture deductions, except that the information is provided through written sentences, not through pictures. A rule is presented, such as, "The people who are running will go to Japan," and a series of sentences tells the children that the boss is running, Boo is sitting, Jean is standing, and so on. The children write the names of people who will go to Japan.

If the comprehension activities in *Reading Mastery,* Grade 1 are presented adequately to the children, even those children who enter the program with low language skills will finish the program with the comprehension skills that are required for taking tests and for extracting new information from textbooks.

TEACHING THE EXERCISES IN *READING MASTERY,* GRADE 1

The remainder of the guide deals with the specific exercises, or formats, that you will present. The more critical exercises are presented, with information about how to teach each exercise and how to correct the more frequent mistakes.

THE PROGRAM BLOCKS

The *Reading Mastery,* Grade 1 program is divided into three blocks. Each block has discrete objectives, although there is carryover from block to block. The *Spelling Presentation Book* (lessons 1–160) corresponds to Block One and Block Two.

Block One: The Firming Block (Lessons 1–39)

The major objectives of this block are
- To firm the children in skills that have been presented in the *Reading Mastery,* Grade K program. The firming consists of reviewing the sounds (symbol identification), working on words that are particularly difficult, introducing some new vocabulary, and expanding the comprehension activities introduced in *Reading Mastery,* Grade K.
- To introduce procedures for rereading vocabulary words.
- To introduce the individual fluency checkouts and other in-program tests.

Block Two: The Vowel Mechanics Block (Lessons 40–80)

The major thrusts of this block are
- To firm sound combinations that involve vowels *(ar, al, ou)*
- To teach letter names for the vowels *(a, e, i, o, u)*
- To teach and apply the vowel rule to words with a final *e (made)*
- To teach discrimination between final *e* words and those without a final *e (made-mad)*
- To read some words in which the macron (long line) has been removed from the vowels *(she, store)*
- To disjoin some of the sound combinations that were taught in *Reading Mastery,* Grade K *(th, sh, ing).*

Block Three: The Textbook Preparation Block (Lessons 81–160)

This block, perhaps the most important in the program, has three objectives:
- To introduce traditional textbook print
- To expand comprehension tasks
- To prepare the children for the kinds of informational reading required by textbooks in various subject areas.

Starting at lesson 86, the children read from completely traditional orthography. More of the stories are information-oriented. Some science information is introduced in Worksheet activities. The Worksheet activities also contain deduction tasks that prepare the children for the kind of logical analysis that is assumed by textbooks.

BLOCK ONE

The Firming Block (Lessons 1–39)

Schedule of Activities for Daily Lessons
- Sounds review (letters identified by sounds, not by letter names)
- Reading vocabulary words
- Story reading and teacher-directed comprehension activities
- Worksheet activities (some teacher-directed, some independent)
- Individual Fluency Checkouts: Rate/Accuracy

The sounds pronunciation guide is on the inside back cover of this guide.

The sounds track contains two formats.

Sounds Format (Lessons 1 and 11)

The first format appears in lessons 1 and 11, the two entry points for the *Reading Mastery,* Grade 1 program.

Critical Behaviors

1. In step *b,* tell the children the rule about their performance ("When I touch it, you say it. Keep on saying it as long as I touch it"). Say the rule quickly, and in a natural way.

2. In step *c,* point to the first sound and say "Get ready." Then touch the sound. The children are to begin saying the sound as soon as you touch it. They are to continue saying it as long as you touch it.

Rules about Pointing and Touching (Sounds)

1. When pointing, hold your finger about an inch from the page, just below the sound you will touch.

2. Be careful not to cover the sound with your point—all children must be able to see it.

3. Say "Get ready" after you have pointed to the sound.

4. Pause for one second.

5. Touch just below the sound.

Note: The interval between the end of "Get ready" and the touch must be timed exactly the same for all tasks so that the children know exactly when you will touch the sound. If you keep the interval between the end of "Get ready" and the touch constant, there will be far fewer "leading" mistakes (which occur when one child in the group responds before the others and "leads" them with the appropriate response).

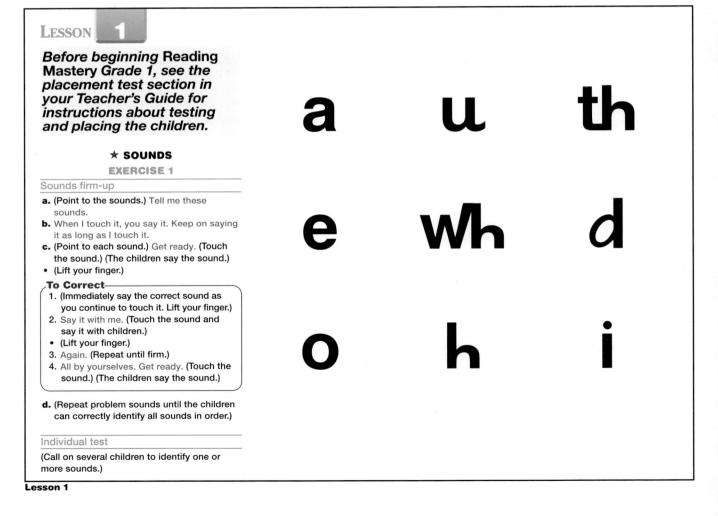

LESSON 1

Before beginning **Reading Mastery** *Grade 1, see the placement test section in your Teacher's Guide for instructions about testing and placing the children.*

★ SOUNDS

EXERCISE 1

Sounds firm-up

a. (Point to the sounds.) Tell me these sounds.

b. When I touch it, you say it. Keep on saying it as long as I touch it.

c. (Point to each sound.) Get ready. (Touch the sound.) (The children say the sound.)
- (Lift your finger.)

To Correct
1. (Immediately say the correct sound as you continue to touch it. Lift your finger.)
2. Say it with me. (Touch the sound and say it with children.)
- (Lift your finger.)
3. Again. (Repeat until firm.)
4. All by yourselves. Get ready. (Touch the sound.) (The children say the sound.)

d. (Repeat problem sounds until the children can correctly identify all sounds in order.)

Individual test

(Call on several children to identify one or more sounds.)

a   u   th

e   wh   d

o   h   i

Lesson 1

6. Do not cover the sound when you touch it.

7. If the sound is a continuous one—such as *a, m, s, r,* and *o,* which can be pronounced until you run out of breath—touch the sound for 2 seconds (two slow beats).

   If the sound is a stop sound such as *d, t, p,* and *c,* which can be pronounced for only an instant, touch the sound for only an instant.

8. Quickly look up at the children an instant after touching the sound.

9. Move your finger quickly and decisively from the page after touching the sound.

Corrections for Inappropriate Responses to Your Touch

There are two basic types of mistakes that you will probably encounter on this format. The first is an inappropriate response to your touch.

- An inappropriate response to your touch is delaying before saying the sound. (You touch the sound; a moment or two later, some of the children respond.)
- Another inappropriate response is responding before you touch the sound.
- Another is continuing to respond after you have released your touch.

To correct inappropriate responses to your touch:

1. Tell the children what they did. You're early, or You're late, or You didn't say it when I touched it, or I stopped touching it, but you kept saying it. Watch my finger. Get ready. Touch. Children respond as you touch.

2. Repeat the signal until the children are firm.

3. Now you're watching my finger. Let's try it again. Then go on to the next sound.

PRACTICE this correction with another adult, using exercise 1 on page 16 of this guide. The adult who plays the role of the child is to make each of these mistakes: coming in early, coming in late, holding the sound after you have released.

The correction above deals with inappropriate responses to your touch. The other major type of correction deals with misidentification of sounds.

Corrections for Sound-Identification Errors

The correction for sound-identification errors appears in a box in lessons 1 to 13. Use this correction through lesson 38. The correction consists of a model, lead, and test.

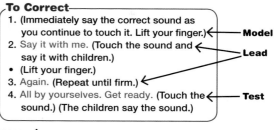

Lesson 1

After lesson 38, the following simplified correction may be used. Notice that the lead step is dropped.

1. *Model:* As soon as you hear a misidentification, say the correct sound loudly, so that all children in the group hear it said the right way.

2. *Test the children:* Your turn. Get ready. Pause one second. Then touch the sound. Listen to the children's responses.

If you are in doubt about the way any child is pronouncing the sound, give the child an individual turn to say the sound.

Note that after correcting a sound-identification error, *you return to the first sound on the page and repeat all of the sounds in order. If children make errors, correct errors. Then return to the first sound again. Continue until the children can correctly identify all sounds in order.*

PRACTICE correcting sound-identification errors. Work with another adult who plays the role of the child. The adult is to make identification errors when you touch some of the sounds on the format on page 16. Remember to respond as soon as you hear an error. (When working with children, you want all of the children in the group to hear the correct identification, not an incorrect one.)

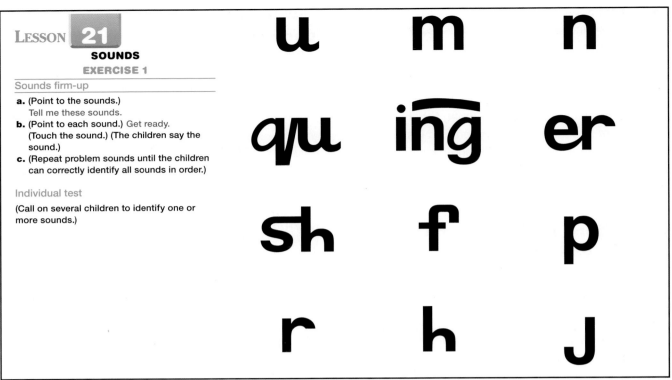

LESSON 21

SOUNDS

EXERCISE 1

Sounds firm-up

a. (Point to the sounds.)
   Tell me these sounds.
b. (Point to each sound.) Get ready.
   (Touch the sound.) (The children say the sound.)
c. (Repeat problem sounds until the children can correctly identify all sounds in order.)

Individual test

(Call on several children to identify one or more sounds.)

Sounds Format (Lesson 21)

In lesson 21, a simplified variation of the sounds format is introduced. This format involves an abbreviated teacher direction ("Tell me these sounds." Point to the first sound. "Get ready . . .").

Note that the correction procedure is not specified in this format; however, the procedures discussed on page 17 should be followed to correct any inappropriate responses to touching and any errors in sound identification.

Track Development

Near the end of Block One (which ends with lesson 39), increasing emphasis is placed on vowels in the Sounds track. The reason is that Block Two deals with vowel mechanics. Make sure the children are quite firm on all vowels, particularly in lessons 38 and 39.

Sound-Combination Review
(Lesson 34)

Beginning in lesson 34, the children review sound combinations as part of their sound-identification activity. Note that the combinations that appear in the sound-combination review have already been taught in reading-vocabulary exercises. (See page 23.)

Two sound combinations are introduced in Block One. They are *al* and *ar.* The sound-combination format appears below.

Critical Behaviors

1. In step *a,* describe the task to the children, telling them to get ready to tell the sound the letter combinations make.

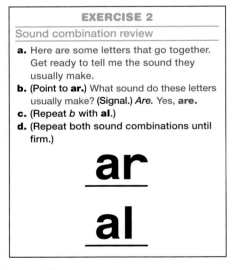

EXERCISE 2

Sound combination review

a. Here are some letters that go together. Get ready to tell me the sound they usually make.
b. (Point to **ar.**) What sound do these letters usually make? (Signal.) *Are.* Yes, **are.**
c. (Repeat *b* with **al.**)
d. (Repeat both sound combinations until firm.)

$$\underline{ar}$$

$$\underline{al}$$

2. In step *b,* point to *ar* and say, "What sound do these letters usually make?"

- When pointing, hold your finger about an inch from the page, just below the middle of *ar.* Be careful not to cover parts of either sound.
- Say, "What sound do these letters usually make?" Do not move your finger as you say this.
- Pause one second after you say the last word in your question *(make).*
- Touch just below the middle of *ar:*

ar

Note: The interval between the end of your question and your touch must be the same interval used between the end of "Get ready" and your touch in the sound-identification format on page 16.

- Touch under the sound combination for only an instant. (Use the same touching procedures you use for stop sounds.) Children are to say the sound combination *ar* quickly. They are not to drag it out.

3. Repeat step *b* of the format for the sound combination *al* (pronounced "all").

- Point to *al.* As you point, say "What sound do these letters usually make?" Continue to point for one second.
- Then touch just under the middle of *al.* Touch for only an instant. The children respond *all* the moment you touch under the combination.

Corrections

Children make inappropriate responses to your touching. They may also make identification mistakes.

Correct inappropriate responses to the touch using the procedures described on page 17.

If children confuse the combinations (calling *ar* "all,") follow this correction.

1. As quickly as possible, tell the sound combination.

2. Point to the last letter in the combination (*l* in *al* or *r* in *ar*). Say: Tell me this sound.

3. If response is not firm, point to the sound and say: Again, and touch the sound. Repeat until the children are firm on identifying the sound.

4. Point under the combination. What sound do these letters usually make? (Step *b* in format.)

5. Pause one second. Then touch just under the middle of the sound combination . . . Yes, arr. Note that you stress the *rrr* sound to tie in with the correction procedure.

6. Repeat steps 2 through 5 above for the other sound combination, *al.*

If the children fail to respond when you touch the sound combination (step 5), tell them the sound the letters usually make. "Are." Then repeat step *b.* "What sound do these letters usually make?"

Repeat both sound combinations until the children are firm on both.

Note: The first step in <u>all</u> corrections is to tell the children the correct answer. If the children miss a sound, the first step is to tell them the correct sound. If the children miss a word, the first step is to tell them the correct word.

In Block One, the children read fifteen to twenty-six words a day in the reading-vocabulary activities. The reading-vocabulary formats begin in lesson 1 and continue every day through lesson 160. Each of the formats requires a different set of presentation steps.

Sound-Out-First Format (Lesson 1)

In Lesson 1, the basic sound-out-first format appears. This format continues through lesson 82.

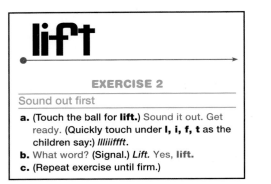

EXERCISE 2

Sound out first

a. (Touch the ball for **lift.**) Sound it out. Get ready. (Quickly touch under **l, i, f, t** as the children say:) *llliiiffft.*
b. What word? (Signal.) *Lift.* Yes, **lift.**
c. (Repeat exercise until firm.)

Lesson 2

Critical Behaviors

The exercise head for exercise 2 indicates what the children do in this format. They sound it out first. Note the exercise headings. They are quick reminders of the type of exercises you will present.

1. In step *a,* touch the ball for *lift* and say, "Sound it out." (Pause.) "Get ready." Quickly touch under *l, i, f, t* as children say, *llliiiffft.*

- Do not give the children the instruction "Sound it out" until you are touching the ball.

- Touch the ball so that you do not cover the first letter of the word.

- After saying "Sound it out," pause. Then say, "Get ready." The purpose of the pause is to allow the children time to look at the word and figure out what they will say.

- Keep your finger on the ball until *after* you have said "Get ready." Pause for one second. (This is the same pause interval used on sound-identification tasks.)

- Move quickly to each letter and stop at each letter. Hold under the *l, i,* and *f* for at least one second each. Hold under the *t* for only an instant. Then move quickly to the end of the

arrow. The children respond, *llliiiffft.*

- After you reach the end of the arrow, return to the ball of the arrow. Say, "What word?" Pause one second. Then slash from the ball to the end of the arrow. The children respond, *lift.* Remember, first you talk—then you signal. Practice this timing. Start with your finger on the ball. Keep your finger on the ball as you say, "What word?" and pause one second. Signal by slashing along the arrow.

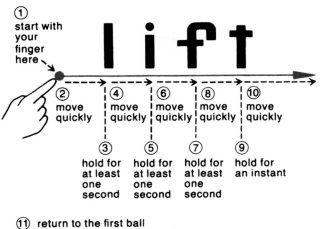

① start with your finger here
② move quickly
④ move quickly
⑥ move quickly
⑧ move quickly
⑩ move quickly
③ hold for at least one second
⑤ hold for at least one second
⑦ hold for at least one second
⑨ hold for an instant

⑪ return to the first ball
⑫ quickly move along the arrow for the say-it-fast signal

Note: Step *a* of the format indicates which symbols you touch and the response the children are to produce for each sound. For the word *lift,* there are three *lll*'s in the response, indicating that the children say this sound for at least one second. There is one *t,* which means that the sound is produced for only an instant. The sound *t* is a stop sound.

PRACTICE moving under the letters in the word *lift.* Remember to move quickly. If you are too slow, the children won't know exactly when to respond. The result will be some children responding before others and leading them.

2. In step *b* of the format (after the children have already sounded out the word), you ask "What word?"

- Before asking "What word?", return to the ball. Hold your finger on the ball as you ask "What word?"

- Then pause one second (the same interval used for other signals).

- Quickly slash to the right along the arrow—an indication that the children are to give a fast response. As you slash, the children are to say the word *"lift"* at a normal speaking rate.
- After the children identify the word, you say "Yes, lift." This step is critical. Make sure that every child in the group hears the word pronounced the right way.

3. If the children are not perfectly firm on steps *a* and *b* of the format, repeat steps *a* and *b* until all children are responding on signal and producing appropriate responses.

Corrections for Sound-Out-First Format

The children are not to pause between the sounds of the word. If you say the word *lift* very slowly, you will say it in the way they are to sound it out. They are not to say *lll—iii—fff—t.* There must be no pause between the letters (*llliiiffft*).

To correct pausing mistakes, present a model, lead, and test:

1. *Model.* Touch the ball of the arrow. My turn. I can sound it out. Get ready. Move under each sound as you say *llliiiffft.*

2. *Lead.* Touch the ball of the arrow. Do it with me. Sound it out. Get ready. Move under each sound as you and the children say *llliiiffft.*

3. *Test.* Touch the ball of the arrow. All by yourselves. Sound it out. Get ready. Move under each sound as the children say *llliiiffft.*

4. Repeat the test step (step 3) until the children are firm.

5. Then touch the ball of the arrow. Say: What word? and quickly slash to the right. Children say *lift.*

To correct sound-identification errors in step a, present a model and a test:

1. *Model.* As soon as you hear a sound misidentification, say the correct sound loudly.

2. *Test.* Point to the sound. What sound? Pause one second. Touch the sound.

3. Say: Let's sound out this word again. Return to the ball of the arrow and repeat step *a* of the format.

Corrections for step *b*

In step *b* of the format, the children may say the word slowly; or mispronounce the word.

To correct mistakes in which the children do not say the word quickly:

1. Say: Say it fast. (Signal.) Praise children who say it fast. Repeat step 1 until children are firm.

2. Touch the ball of the arrow. Say: Yes, what word? Pause one second. Then slash right.

3. Repeat steps *a* and *b* of the format.

To correct mispronunciations:

1. Listen carefully to the way the children say the word, particularly the ending sounds. Children often leave off endings or slur them.

2. If you are in doubt, call on several children in the group and ask: What word? Beth, what word? . . . Dan, what word?

3. If you hear an incorrect pronunciation, immediately say the word the right way. Lift. What word, Dan? Everybody, what word?

4. Repeat steps *a* and *b* of the format.

The sound-out-first format below is the same format that was used to present *lift.* The sounding out is different because the word *clap* begins with a stop sound.

EXERCISE 3

Sound out first

a. (Touch the ball for **clap.**) Sound it out. Get ready. (Quickly touch under **c, l, a, p** as the children say:) *clllaaap.*
b. What word? (Signal.) *Clap.* Yes, **clap.**
c. (Repeat exercise until firm.)

Lesson 2

The children's response indicated in step *a* (clllaaap) specifies the *c* and *p* are stop sounds and the other sounds (*l* and *a*) are continuous and are to be held for one second each.

Critical Behaviors

1. After saying "Sound it out . . . Get ready" in step *a,* pause one second. Then move very quickly to *c* and to *l.* Touch under *c* for only an instant.

2. Children may pause between *c* and *l.* If they do, repeat step *a* until the children are saying *"clll"* without pausing (or with a very slight pause).

PRACTICE moving under the sounds in *clap.*

Corrections

At step *b,* the children may say "lap" instead of "clap."

To correct:
Point to *c.* Say: First you say **c.**
Point to *lap.* Say: Then you say **lap.**
Point to *c.* Say: What do you say first? The children respond *c.*
Point to *lap.* Say: Then what do you say? The children respond *lap.*
Touch ball of arrow. Say: Get ready. Move quickly to *c.* The children say *c.*
Slash under *lap.* Children say *lap.*
Quickly touch ball of arrow. Say: What word? Slash right. The children say *clap.*

If the children fail to respond, tell them the word. Then repeat the correction.

Below is the same sound-out-first format. This time it is used to present a word that has a long line over a vowel and a small letter.

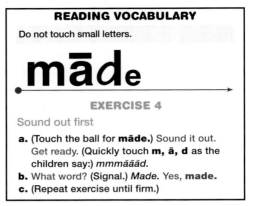

READING VOCABULARY

Do not touch small letters.

EXERCISE 4

Sound out first

a. (Touch the ball for **māde.**) Sound it out. Get ready. (Quickly touch **m, ā, d** as the children say:) *mmmāāād.*
b. What word? (Signal.) *Made.* Yes, **made.**
c. (Repeat exercise until firm.)

Lesson 7

Critical Behaviors

1. When sounding out words with small letters, do not touch the small letters. The teacher instructions in step *a* indicate that you touch under *m, ā, d.* You do not touch under the small *e.* The children do not pronounce the *e.*

Note that small letters may appear in the middle of some words:

mēan   trāin

The children's response for the sounding out indicated in step *a* shows that the children say *mmm* and *āāā* (long a). These are continuous sounds. The *d* is a stop sound, held for only an instant.

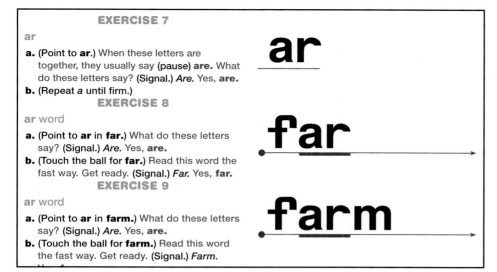

EXERCISE 7

ar

a. (Point to **ar**.) When these letters are together, they usually say (pause) **are**. What do these letters say? (Signal.) *Are.* Yes, **are**.
b. (Repeat *a* until firm.)

EXERCISE 8

ar word

a. (Point to **ar** in **far**.) What do these letters say? (Signal.) *Are.* Yes, **are**.
b. (Touch the ball for **far**.) Read this word the fast way. Get ready. (Signal.) *Far.* Yes, **far**.

EXERCISE 9

ar word

a. (Point to **ar** in **farm**.) What do these letters say? (Signal.) *Are.* Yes, **are**.
b. (Touch the ball for **farm**.) Read this word the fast way. Get ready. (Signal.) *Farm.*

Lesson 2

Sound-Combination Format (Lesson 2)

In Lesson 2, the basic sound-combination format is introduced. The heading of the exercise indicates the sound combination involved: *ar.*

- In exercise 7, the teacher identifies what the letters say, and tests the children: "What do these letters say?"
- In exercise 8, the teacher points to the bar that is under *ar* and asks, "What do these letters say?" The teacher then tells the children to read the word the fast way.
- In exercise 9, the teacher points to the bar under *ar* in the word *farm* and asks, "What do these letters say?"
- The teacher then tells the children to read the word the fast way.

Critical Behaviors for Exercise 7

1. Point between *a* and *r* before you say, "When these letters are together, they usually say (pause) *are*."

2. Remember to pause before saying *are* in the above statement.

3. After you ask "What do these letters say?" signal by touching just under the middle of *ar.* (See pages 18 and 19.)

4. Repeat step 3 until firm. Make sure that children are pronouncing *are* appropriately.

Critical Behaviors for Exercise 8

As soon as children are firm on exercise 7, move quickly to step *a* in exercise 8.

1. Point to the bar under *ar* in *far.* Move your finger back and forth along the bar. As you point to the bar, ask, "What do these letters say?"

2. Pause one second. Signal by touching the bar between *a* and *r.* When you touch the bar, the children are to respond, "Are."

3. Next, touch the ball of the arrow. Say "Read this word the fast way." Pause 2 seconds. "Get ready." Signal by slashing quickly along the arrow to the right. As you slash, children are to say "far," at a normal speaking rate.

Critical Behavior for Exercise 9

Exercise 9 involves the same steps as exercise 8.

PRACTICE presenting Exercises 7, 8, and 9 in order. Remember to move quickly from exercise to exercise.

Corrections

The children may fail to identify the words in exercise 8 or exercise 9.
To correct:
1. Tell the children the word.
2. Touch the ball of the arrow. Sound it out. Get ready.
3. Move under *f ar m* as the children say *fffarmmm.* Note that the children are to identify the *ar* combination as *are,* not as *aaarrr* or *air.*
- When moving under *ar,* go to the middle of the bar, between *a* and *r.*
- Do not hold under *ar* for more time than the children need to say *are.* (An instant.)

- If children misidentify *ar* in sounding out, repeat exercise 7 of the format. Then repeat the sounding out.

4. After children have sounded out the word appropriately, return to the ball of the arrow. Say: **What word?** Slash quickly to the right as children say *farm*.

5. Return to exercise 7 on the format page and repeat all exercises in order until the children are firm on every step.

Hard-Words Format (lesson 4)

Beginning in lesson 3, the children are presented with lists of "hard words." These are words that have been presented in the program but often give the poor reader some trouble. "Hard word" exercises appear in lessons 3, 4, 8, 9, 13, 18, 32, and 47. The initial hard-word exercises are divided into two parts. First, the children read words from the teacher's presentation book; then the children *individually* read a column of words from their reader.

Below is the teacher presentation of the hard words exercise from lesson 4.

READING HARD WORDS
EXERCISE 4

Hard words

You'll present rewards in this exercise.

a. (Point to the hard words in your book.) Today, you're going to read these hard words. First you'll read them in my book. Then you'll read some of them in your reader. If you can read all of the words in a column without making a mistake, you'll get_____. (Reward the children with stars, points, etc.)

b. (Point to **here**.) Reading the fast way. (Pause two seconds.) Get ready. (Signal.) *Here.*

c. (Repeat *b* for the remaining words that appear on pages 18, 19, and 20.)

To Correct
1. Everybody, sound out the word. (Touch each sound as the children sound out the word.)
2. What word? (Signal.)

d. (Repeat each column on pages 18, 19, and 20 until the children can identify each word without making a mistake.)

hēre
her
whēre
wēre
hē
the
shē

āte
at
when
whȳ
they
then
there
thēse
thōse
ēven
every
very

didn't
dōn't
fōr
of
do
clap
did
are
farm
barn
yard

Lesson 4

Presenting Hard Words from the Presentation Book

1. The procedure for presenting each word in the Presentation Book is to touch the ball of the arrow and say, "Reading the fast way."

2. Pause two seconds to allow the children to look at the word. During this time, keep your finger on the ball of the arrow.

3. Say "Get ready." Pause one second. Then quickly slash right along the arrow. As you slash, the children are to say the word at a normal speaking rate.

Corrections

Correct all identification errors by first saying the word correctly. Then have the children sound out the word. Finally, have the children answer the question "What word?"

1. Tell the children the word.

2. Touch the ball of the arrow. Say: Everybody, sound out the word.

3. Move quickly under each sound as the children say the sounds without pausing between the sounds.

4. Return to the ball of the arrow after the word has been sounded out.

5. Say: What word? Pause one second. Quickly slash right along the arrow as children say the word at a normal speaking rate.

6. Return to the first word in the column. Say: Starting over.

Note: The children are to identify any sound combination as a combination, not as individual letters. When sounding out *barn,* they identify *ar* as "are." If they sound out the word *wall,* they identify the *al* as "all." Any sound combination that is taught is always sounded out as a combination.

Repeat the hard words in the Teacher Presentation Book until the children are firm on every column.

Hard Words in Reader (Lesson 4)

In the second part of the initial hard-words exercise, the children read words from their readers.

Critical Behaviors

This exercise involves individual reading. Each child in the group reads every word in one of the columns. You proceed from one column to the next in order, calling on a different child to read each column.

Keep track of the children who miss more than one word when reading a column.

★ HARD WORDS IN READER 4

Exercise 5 is a test of reading accuracy. Tally all reading errors on a separate sheet.

EXERCISE 5

Hard words in reader

a. Keep your reader open to page 6. ✔
b. These words are the same hard words you just read.
c. (Call on a child.) Read the words in the first column. Start at the top and go down the column. Everybody, touch the words that are being read. Raise your hand if you hear a mistake.
d. (Call on another child to read the second column.)
e. (Give each child a turn at reading one column of words. Praise the children who read each word in the column without making a mistake. Children who make a mistake must repeat the word until firm.)

To Correct
1. (Immediately say the correct word.)
2. (Tell the child who made the mistake:) Touch that word. (Pause.) What word?
3. (Then tell the child:) Now go back to the top of the column and read the words again.

f. (If the children average more than one mistake, do not proceed to lesson 5. See the Teacher's Guide for details.)

Lesson 4   Presentation Book

---

did	thōse	are
clap	thēse	farm
do	there	yard
of	then	her
fōr	whȳ	hēre
dōn't	when	at
didn't	were	āte
very	where	hē
every	her	shē
ēven	hēre	thē

Procedures for Firm-up on Hard-Words Days

- Keep all children in the group until each child has had a first turn. Then dismiss children who made no mistakes in reading their column of hard words. Instruct them to do their seatwork for the lesson.
- Keep the other children and work with them. The procedures are outlined below.

Present the following firm-up procedure for children who make more than one mistake on a column of words.

1. Instruct the children who miss more than one word to study all the words on the page until they can read every word without making a mistake. Allow the children about two minutes to study the words.

2. Direct each child to read all the hard words individually to you. Tell the child not to hurry, to point to each word, and to "read the word the fast way" (without sounding out). *It is very important for the children to point to each word as they read it.*

- If a child misidentifies a word, tell the child to sound out the word and then answer the question, "What word?" Then tell the child to return to the first word on the page and read all of the words in order.

- If a child misidentifies a sound or sound combination when sounding out a word, tell the child the sound or sound combination. Then have the child sound out the word again. After the sounding out is firm, ask, "What word?"
- If a child reads all words without making mistakes, praise the child for good reading. Do not scold the child for having missed words before.
- If a child makes more than one mistake in reading all words on the page, write each word on a card, mix up the cards, and present the cards to the child. A child who is considered firm on the words can go through the stack two times without making mistakes. *Remember to write all the words with the same letters and lines that appear in the Reading Mastery program.* For example, write *here* this way

$$hēre$$

and *where* this way—

$$where$$

Track Development

Use the firm-up procedures above for every lesson that contains hard words except lesson 3 (the first hard-words day). Note that on later hard-word days, beginning with lesson 8, the hard words appear only in the reader, not in the Teacher Presentation Book. On hard word days, there is no other reading vocabulary and there are no stories. Use these hard-word days to diagnose specific problems and correct those problems. The minimum firm-up is specified above. If it is apparent that some children are weak on sounds, on sounding out, or on reading the fast way, a more elaborate firming procedure would be implied. Children should not proceed in the program if they are not firm on all hard words and on the operations they have been taught for reading words. (This is especially important on test lessons 4, 9, and 13.)

Read-the-Fast-Way Format
(Lesson 5)

The read-the-fast-way format begins in lesson 1 and continues through lesson 160. It is the most common reading-vocabulary format in the *Reading Mastery, Grade 1* program. The read-the-fast-way format for lesson 5 is shown on page 28.

Do not touch small letters.

Get ready to read all the words on this page without making a mistake.

EXERCISE 5

Read the fast way

a. Read these words the fast way.
b. (Touch the ball for **that**. Pause two seconds.) Get ready. (Signal.) *That*. Yes, **that**.
c. (Repeat *b* for **girls, gōing, talking, shē, them, thōse,** and **this**.)

that
girls
gōing
talking
shē
them
thōse
this

(Repeat any troublesome words.)

Individual test

(Call on individual children. Each child reads a different word.)

Lesson 5

Critical Behaviors

The exercise heading for exercise 5 indicates that the children "read the fast way."

1. In step *a,* you give instructions about how the words are to be read. Point to the words that are to be read. (Other words may appear on the page that are not to be read the fast way.)

2. In step *b,* touch the ball for the first word, *that*. Pause two seconds. Then say "Get ready." Pause the standard interval. Then signal by slashing right along the arrow.

Note: For some groups, the two-second pause after you touch the ball of the arrow may not be needed. The children in these groups can often perform with only a one-second pause, or perhaps a half-second pause. You can reduce the length of the pause if the group seems firm; however, most teachers err in the direction of not allowing the children enough time to figure out the words before requiring the children to read the fast way. As a result, some children in the group will perform, but others learn to respond late and to copy the responses of the leaders.

Individual Turns

After children have read all the words on the page, present the individual test. Here are the general rules for individual tests:

1. Do not present individual tests until the group seems firm on every word. If you hear members of the group make mistakes or come in late, do not present individual turns. Instead, firm the *group* on all words.

2. Sample the higher and middle-performing children in the group. Also *call on every lower performer* (any child whose performance is questionable).

3. Seat children who perform poorly on individual tests directly in front of you so that you can listen to their responses when the group is responding. If they are far from you, you won't be able to hear what they are saying during the group responses.

Corrections for Read the Fast Way (Group Turn)

If children miss any words in steps *b* or *c:*

1. Tell the children the word.

2. Touch the ball of the arrow. Say: Everybody, sound out the word.

3. Then ask them: What word?

4. Return to the first word in the column and present all words in order.

Sounding Out Slightly Irregular Words (Example: *those*)

When sounding out *those,* they would sound it out with a *sss* sound, not with a *zzz* sound. The letter is *s* and the sound is *sss* (*thththōōōsss*). They pronounce the word as "thōze."

Sounding Out Words with Sound Combinations (Example: *arm*)

A word such as *arm* would be sounded out "armmm" with the *ar* pronounced quickly as "are." This word involves a sound combination that *has been taught.* If a word contains a combination that has not been taught, the children are to say the only sound they have been taught for each of the letters in the combination. After they have been taught *al* (which hasn't taken place yet at lesson 5), they would sound out *salt* as *sssalt* with *al* pronounced as "all." Before *al* is taught, however, they would sound out the word "sssaaalllt," identifying the sound *a* as "aaa" and the sound *l* as "lll."

Sounding Out Highly Irregular Words

In the read-the-fast-way format from lesson 5, the words *girls* and *talking* are highly irregular, which means that the pronunciation of these words does not closely correspond to the way in which the words are sounded out. The rule about irregulars in Block One is: *The children are to say the sound for each full-sized symbol in the word.*

When sounding out *girls,* the children say "giiirrrlllsss," not "guuurrrlllzzz." (There is no *u* or *z* in the written word.)

If children say "guuurrrlllzzz" instead of "giiirrrlllsss," use this correction:

To correct:

1. Stop the children as soon as you hear a sound pronunciation error. Point under the mispronounced sound and say the sound correctly as quickly as possible.

2. Touch under the mispronounced sound. Say: What sound?

3. Return to the sounding-out task. Touch the ball of the arrow. Say: Sound it out. (Pause.) Get ready. (Pause.) Move under each letter as children say *giiirrrlllsss.* Repeat sounding out until firm.

4. Then ask: What word? The children respond *girls.* Yes, **girls.**

    When the children answer the question "What word?" they say the irregular word as it is normally pronounced *(gurlz).*

    If children try to pronounce the irregular word in the same way they sound it out, tell them: That's how we **sound out** the word. But this is how we **say** the word: **gurlz.** Then have the children again sound out the word and answer the question What word?

Correction for Read the Fast Way (Individual Turn)

If a child misses a word on an individual test, tell the child the word. Then tell the child to read other words. The individual test provides information about which children have difficulty and which skills are deficient.

PRACTICE sounding out every word on the page. Make sure that you can say the appropriate sound for each letter indicated in the words. (Check the pronunciation guide on the inside back cover.)

Last-Part, First-Part Format

In lesson 10, the last-part, first-part format is introduced. This format is used for words that involve initial consonant blends that are difficult.

EXERCISE 4

Last part, first part

a. (Cover **s**. Point to **wim**.) Read this part of the word the fast way. (Pause two seconds.) Get ready. (Signal.) *Wim.* Yes, **wim.**

b. (Uncover **s**. Point to **s**.) First you say **sss.** (Move your finger quickly under **wim**.) Then you say (pause) **wim.**

c. (Touch the ball for **swim**.) Get ready. (Move to **s**, then quickly along the arrow.) *Ssswim.*

d. Say it fast. (Signal.) *Swim.*

• Yes, what word? (Signal.) *Swim.*

• Yes, **swim.** Good reading.

e. (Repeat *c* and *d* until firm.)

Lesson 10

Critical Behaviors

1. In step *a*, cover *s* and point to *wim.*
• Practice covering *s* so that you do not conceal other parts of the word.
• When you point to *wim,* run your finger under the letters *w-i-m.*
• Say, "Read this part of the word the fast way."
• Pause two seconds. Point under the letter *w.* Say, "Get ready." Then slash under *wim.* After the children respond *wim,* say, "Yes, wim."

2. In step *b*, uncover *s.* Point to *s* and say, "First you say *sss.*" Move your finger quickly under *wim* as you say, "Then you say *wim.*"

3. In step *c*, touch the ball for *swim* and say, "Get ready." Then move quickly under *s* and hold as the children say "sss." Then quickly slash under *wim* as the children continue to say "swim." The children's response to the word is "ssswim."

4. In step *d*, return to the ball and say, "Say it fast." Signal by slashing under the word. The children say "swim."

Corrections

1. If children are weak in saying *ssswim* in step *c,* repeat steps *b* and *c* until the children are firm.

2. If children are weak in saying the word fast in step *d,* repeat steps *c* and *d* until firm.

PRACTICE this format with another adult. First practice the steps when the person working with you makes no mistakes. Then practice it when the person pauses between the parts, saying "sss—wim" instead of "ssswim."

Listen, Sound-Out Format

In lesson 10, the first listen, sound-out format is introduced. This format is used to introduce irregularly pronounced words. (These are words that are sounded out one way and pronounced another way.) The format is also used to introduce some words that are quite difficult to say fast after they have been sounded out. The format appears from lessons 10 through 80. Generally, a new irregular word will appear in the format one or two times before going into one of the other formats, such as the read-the-fast-way format.

other

EXERCISE 5

Listen, sound out

a. (Point to **other**.) I'll tell you this word. (Pause.) **Other.** What word? (Signal.) *Other.* Yes, **other**.

b. (Touch the ball for **other**.) Sound it out. Get ready. (Quickly touch **o,th,er** as the children say:) *ooothththerrr.*

To Correct

If the children do not say the sounds you point to

1. (Say:) You've got to say the sounds I point to.

2. (Repeat *b* until firm.)

c. What word? (Signal.) *Other.* Yes, **other.**

d. (Repeat *b* and *c* until firm.)

Lesson 10

Critical Behaviors

- In step *a,* tell the children the word and test them on the pronunciation of the word.
- In step *b,* the children sound out the word.

Corrections

The most frequent mistake comes in step *b* when the children say "uuuthththerrr" instead of "oooothththerrr." (Note that the word is irregular only in the pronunciation of the first letter.)

To correct sounding out of irregular words:

1. Stop the children as soon as you hear a sound pronunciation error. Say the word as quickly as possible.

2. Touch under the mispronounced sound. Say: What sound?

3. Then say: You've got to say the sounds I point to.

4. Repeat the sounding out (step *b*) until the children are firm.

Two-Part-Word Format

In lesson 36, the first two-part-word format is introduced. This type of format is used throughout the program to teach the children how to analyze parts of words, including endings. The format requires the teacher to cover the last part of the word as the children read the first part. Then the teacher uncovers the remainder of the word, and the children read the entire word.

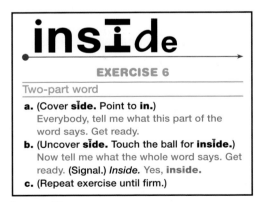

EXERCISE 6

Two-part word

a. (Cover **sĭde**. Point to **in**.)
   Everybody, tell me what this part of the word says. Get ready.
b. (Uncover **sĭde**. Touch the ball for **insĭde**.)
   Now tell me what the whole word says. Get ready. (Signal.) *Inside.* Yes, **inside**.
c. (Repeat exercise until firm.)

Lesson 36

Critical Behaviors

1. In step *a,* cover the last part of the word so that you don't obscure any letter in the first part. (You can cover the ending with a piece of paper if you find it more convenient.)

- With your free hand, point to *in.* (Point slightly below the letter *i.*) Say "Everybody, tell me what this part of the word says. Get ready." Signal by touching between *i* and *n.*

2. In step *b,* uncover the ending of the word. Touch the ball for the word and say "Now tell me what the whole word says." Pause to allow the children to look at the word. "Get ready." Signal by slashing right along the arrow. "Yes, inside."

Corrections for step *a*

In step *a,* the children may make the mistake of telling you the first sound in the word rather than the first part of the word, *in.*

To correct:

1. Underscore *in* with your finger. This is the part I want to know about. Everybody, tell me what this part of the word says. Get ready . . . .

2. Continue with step *b* of the format. Repeat the task until the children are firm.

Corrections for step *b*

In step *b,* the children may make the mistake of failing to identify the whole word appropriately.

To correct:

1. First consider that you may not have given them enough time before saying "Get ready" and signaling. Try step *b* again, this time with a longer pause.

2. If the children still misidentify the word, have them sound out the word and answer the question "What word?"

3. Then return to step *a* of the format and repeat all steps.

Track Development

Not all formats that appear in Block One reading vocabulary are discussed here. There is a format that deals with sound-combination words. Another format, labeled "Read the fast way first," directs children to read the word the fast way and then sound it out. A format labeled "Listen, sound out with me" introduces difficult and irregular words.

If you familiarize yourself with the formats presented in the guide, practice presenting them, and practice the corrections, you will be able to present the basic reading vocabulary tasks so children experience minimum problems.

Procedures for Rereading Vocabulary Words

In most lessons in Block One, children read fifteen to thirty-five words, arranged in columns on two or three pages. Instructions for directing the children to reread the words appear at the end of each page. For all but the last page in the reading-vocabulary exercises, the teacher repeats any troublesome words, and then presents individual tests by calling on different children to read a word from the page.

The last page of each reading-vocabulary lesson directs the teacher to call on individual children to read a *column* of words.

All words should be read the fast way on the individual test. If the column contains only one or two words, the child should read additional words from an adjacent column.

Praise children who read all words with no errors. Encourage children whose performance is improving. Column reading samples each child's reading progress. If a child is tested at least several times a week, the teacher receives good information on the child's progress.

After the children have completed the sounds and reading vocabulary activities of each lesson, they read a story. The teacher directs the reading and presents comprehension questions that are specified in the teacher-presentation script for the lesson.

For the story reading, the children should be sitting at desks, at a table, or on chairs. If they are on chairs, the children should have lapboards.

Rules for Setting Up the Reading Group

1. Seat the children so that the lowest performing children (including any children who have tendencies to act up) are directly in front of you. The better-performing children should be seated on the ends of the group.

2. Pass out storybooks to every child.

3. Children are to open their storybooks to the specified page. They are not to look ahead to the story picture (if the picture is not on the page where the story begins).

4. Children are to lay books flat on lapboards or desks. (If books are flat, you can see where the children are reading. If children hold books up, they cannot point to the words they read, and you cannot see where they are reading.)

Story-Reading Format from Lesson 2
(Questions on Second Reading)

Following are the steps for story reading:

1. The children read the title a word at a time. Children read the title the fast way (without sounding out each word before identifying it).

2. Next, the children read the story the fast way, a word at a time. The title and first three sentences are read in unison, with the teacher tapping as a signal for each word.

3. After the children have read the first three sentences, the teacher calls on individual children, each to read one of the following sentences. From time to time, the teacher directs the group to read.

   When the individual children read, the teacher does not tap.

   When the group reads, the teacher taps for each word.

4. The children reread the story after they are firm on the first reading.

STORYBOOK

STORY 2
EXERCISE 12

First reading—title and three sentences

a. (Pass out Storybook 1.)
b. Everybody, open your reader to page 3.
c. Everybody, touch the title. (Check to see that the children are touching under the first word of the title.)
d. I'll tap and you read each word in the title the fast way. Don't sound it out. Just tell me the word.
e. First word. ✔
• (Pause two seconds.) Get ready. (Tap.) (The children read *paint*.)
f. Next word. (Check to see that the children are touching under the next word. Pause two seconds.) Get ready. (Tap.) (The children read *that*.)
g. (Repeat f for the remaining word in the title.)
h. Everybody, say the title. (Signal.) *Paint that nose.* Yes, **paint that nose.**
i. Everybody, get ready to read this story the fast way.
j. First word. ✔
• (Pause two seconds.) Get ready. (Tap.) *A.*
k. Next word. ✔
• (Pause two seconds.) Get ready. (Tap.) *Fat.*
l. (Repeat k for the remaining words in the first three sentences. Have the children reread the first three sentences until firm.)

EXERCISE 13

Remaining sentences

a. I'm going to call on individual children to read a sentence. Everybody, follow along and point to the words. If you hear a mistake, raise your hand.
b. (Call on a child.) Read the next sentence.

To Correct

word-identification errors
(from, for example)
1. That word is **from.** What word? *From.*
2. Go back to the beginning of the sentence and read the sentence again.

c. (Call on another child.) Read the next sentence.
d. (Repeat c for most of the remaining sentences in the story.)
e. (Occasionally have the group read a sentence. When the group is to read, say:) Everybody, read the next sentence. (Pause two seconds. Tap for each word in the sentence. Pause at least two seconds between taps.)

NOTE: Underlined and numbered statements in the following copy of story 2 refer to questions you are to ask the children in exercise 14.

---

pāint that nōse.[1]
a fat dog met a little dog.
the fat dog had a red nōse.[2] the little dog had a red nōse.[3]
    the fat dog said, "I have a red nōse."
    the little dog said, "I wish I did not have a red nōse."[4]
    the fat dog got a can of pāint. hē said, "pāint that nōse."[5]
    sō the little dog did pāint her nōse. shē said, "now this nōse is not red." shē kissed the fat dog on the ēar. now the fat dog has pāint on his ēar.[6]
        the end

EXERCISE 14

Second reading—sentences and questions

a. You're going to read the story again. This time I'm going to ask questions.
b. Starting with the first word of the title. ✔
• Get ready. (Tap as the children read the title.)
c. (Call on a child.) Read the first sentence.
d. (Call on another child.) Read the next sentence.
e. (Repeat d for most of the remaining sentences in the story.)
f. (Occasionally have the group read a sentence.)
g. (After each underlined sentence has been read, present each comprehension question specified below to the entire group.)

[1] What's this story about? (Signal.) *Paint that nose.*
[2] Who had a red nose? (Signal.) *The fat dog.*
[3] Who else had a red nose? (Signal.) *The little dog.*
[4] What did the little dog say? (Signal.) *I wish I did not have a red nose.*
[5] What did he say? (Signal.) *Paint that nose.*
• Who said that? (Signal.) *The fat dog.*
• He told the little dog to paint her own nose.
[6] Where does the fat dog have paint? (Signal.) *On his ear.*
• How did it get there? (The children respond.)

EXERCISE 15

Picture comprehension

a. What do you think you'll see in the picture? (The children respond.)
b. Turn the page and look at the picture.
c. (Ask these questions:)
   1. What is that little dog doing? (Signal.) *Painting her nose.*
   2. What is behind that little dog's ear? (Signal.) *A paintbrush.* Yes, another paintbrush.
   3. Did you ever paint your nose? (The children respond.)
   4. What do you like to paint best? (Let the children comment for ten seconds. Then comment briefly.)

5. On the second reading, the teacher presents comprehension questions. These are specified in the teacher presentation material. A reduced copy of the children's story appears boxed in the Teacher Presentation Book. The sentences about which questions are to be asked are *underlined* and numbered. The questions that the teacher asks are numbered.

6. The last task dealing with the story is picture comprehension. The children refer to the story picture and answer questions.

Critical Behaviors for Exercise 12
(Group Reading of Title and First Three Sentences)

- Steps *e* and *f* of exercise 12 present the basic procedure for directing children to read words the fast way, a word at a time (which means that the children do not read a string of words after a single tap from the teacher; they read one word for one tap.)

1. When you say "First word," the children are to touch under the first word of the title.
- Make sure that the children are not covering part of the word.
- Do not proceed until all children are touching under the appropriate word and until they have a chance to examine the word.

2. Use the same timing for "Get ready," pause, and tap that you used in Reading Vocabulary exercises. It is very important that the timing of the "Get ready . . ." tap is very predictable. If the children know exactly when the signal will come, they will be able to read the word, on signal, without looking up at you. If the timing is not consistent, however, the children will probably have to glance at you and lose some concentration on the word they are trying to read.

3. In step *f*, you say "Next word." This is a signal for the children to touch under the next word. *Do not proceed until you observe all children touching under the appropriate word.*

4. Pause to give the children time to figure out the word. Then say "Get ready . . ." and tap. Children read the word as you tap.

5. Follow the procedure above for all words in the title and in the first three sentences of the story. Repeat the reading of the first three sentences if the group is not firm. Children are to stop at the end of each sentence, keeping their finger under the last word. The reason for this convention is that comprehension questions may be asked at the end of the sentence.

PRACTICE presenting exercise 12 to another adult. Make sure that you follow all of the steps specified above.

Note: If a group is quite strong at reading the story, you may wish to drop some of the structure specified above and to speed up the rate at which the children read words. However, you must gear the rate of story reading to the performance of the lower performers in the group.

Critical Behaviors for Exercise 13
(Individual and Group Reading of Remaining Sentences)

In exercise 13, the children read the remainder of the story.

1. In step *a,* give the children the instructions about what they are to do.

2. In step *b,* call on a child to read the next sentence. The child is to read every word in the sentence the fast way. Children should read at their own rate. Do not tap for each word.
- Encourage the child to read fluently. "Read it as well as you can."
- Do not hurry the child.
- Praise the child for good fluent reading.
- The child is to stop at the end of the sentence.
- Make sure that the other children in the group are following along and pointing to the words being read. (This is an indication that they may be reading the words to themselves.)
- Do not call on the children to read in an order that is predictable. Mix up the order so that any child is prepared to read any sentence (even if the child has just read the preceding sentence).

3. In step *e,* note that you will occasionally call on the entire group to read a sentence. When the group reads, follow the next word-get ready-tap procedure outlined for the reading of the title and the first three sentences (Critical Behaviors for Exercise 12).

Note: If your group of children reads quite fluently and accurately, you may direct each child to read more than one sentence.

Critical Behaviors for Exercise 14
(Individual and Group Reading and Comprehension)

The focus of exercise 14 is on comprehension. You direct the group in the second reading of the story.

1. The group reads the title in unison.

2. Then you call on different children each to read a sentence.

3. As the children read the story you ask specified comprehension questions. These are indicated in the teacher directions for the second reading. The boxed story that appears in the format indicates when different questions are to be presented.

   - The title of the story in the format is underlined and followed by a 1 (<u>paint that nose</u>[1]), which means that you ask question 1 *after the children have read the title.*

   - Question 1 appears in boldface (in the third column of the page). That question is, "What's this story about?" Children say: "Paint that nose."

     Confirm the correct response. "Yes, it's about painting a nose."

   - After the children have read "The fat dog had a red nose" (which is underlined and numbered[2]), you ask question 2. "Who had a red nose?" Children say: "The fat dog."

     Note that there are three basic types of questions presented during the second reading.

Type one. A response that involves a few words. The response for this type of question is always indicated in the text. Often variations of the response that is specified for the question are perfectly acceptable.

Type two. The children repeat a sentence or what somebody said in a quote. (Question 4, for example.) After the children read "The little dog said, 'I wish I did not have a red nose'," the teacher asks, "What did the little dog say?" The answer: "I wish I did not have a red nose." *The children must produce these responses verbatim.* Questions of this type are very important. They help children learn to remember facts and sequences that are presented in stories.

Type three. The children express an opinion or summarize events that were discussed in more than one sentence of the story. For example, the second part of question 6: "How did it get there?" Acceptable answers would include: "That little dog had paint on her nose and she kissed that fat dog." "The little dog kissed the fat dog and the paint got on his ear," and so on. Note that the response to the question, "How did it get there?" is not specified. When you see the words *the children respond,* you may expect more than one correct answer.

If children give an acceptable response to *type one* or *type three* questions, accept the response even if it is not the response specified in the text. For the *type two* questions, however, hold the children to a very firm criterion. Make sure that every child is saying the sentence appropriately and is including every word.

Corrections for Exercise 12
(Group Reading)

If the group misidentifies a word, follow the correction procedure on the page:

- First, tell the correct word. Then ask, "What word?"

- After the group has correctly identified the word, have the children return to the first word of the sentence in which the mistake occurred and read every word in the sentence. Everybody, back to the first word of the sentence and get ready to read it again, the fast way. Check to make sure the children touch the first word of the sentence.

  This procedure is very important. Do not simply correct and go on. Go back to the beginning of the sentence.

Corrections for Exercise 13
(Individual Reading)

If any child misidentifies a word when reading on an individual turn or is incapable of identifying a word, use the same correction procedure as you did for the group reading:

- First, tell the correct word. Then ask, "What word?"

- After the child has correctly identified the word, have the child return to the first word of the sentence in which the mistake occurred and read every word in the sentence.

Note: If you wish, you can call on a child who raised his or her hand to identify the word. Direct the reader to repeat the word, return to the first word of the sentence, and read all the words in the sentence. The rereading of the sentence gives you information about how firm the child actually is and how well the child was able to handle the information given in the correction.

Corrections for Exercise 14
(Comprehension Errors)

In the step *g* of exercise 14, the children answer comprehension questions. They can make many different types of mistakes. Here are the most common mistakes and how to correct them.

Drony Responses

Children may answer questions as if they are reading the answer. For example, after the children read the title, the teacher asks, "What's this story about?" The children respond by saying, "Paint—that—nose."

Correction for Drony Responses

1. Tell the children what they did: You're not reading now. You're talking to me. I'll answer the question. Listen: What's this story about? **Paint that nose.**

2. Test the children. Your turn. What's this story about? Children say, *Paint that nose.*

3. Praise the children. Now you're talking the right way.

4. Provide children with a *model* of an appropriate response. Take note when children use a drony response and model a faster paced voice in directions and signals.

Grammatical Mistakes

Another typical mistake is that the children use inappropriate grammatical structures. For example, the children read: "He went to the store." Teacher asks, "Where did he go?" Children: "He go to the store."

Correction for Grammatical Mistakes

1. Acknowledge that the children got the right information. Yes, that's right.

2. *Model* the appropriate way to answer the question: He **went** to the store.

3. *Test.* Everybody, say that.

Information Mistakes

The children may not be able to say all the words in a long sentence that has been read haltingly. For example, a child reads. "The little dog said, `I wish I did not have a red nose.'" Teacher asks, "What did the little dog say?" Children are unable to say the sentence.

Correction for Information Mistakes

1. Read the sentence to the children at a more normal speaking rate. Listen to the sentence: . . . .

2. Repeat the question. What did the little dog say?

3. If children still have trouble, follow the *model-lead-test* procedure.
   Model: First say what the little dog said.
   Lead: Then say it with the children.
   Test: Then have the children say it without your lead.

4. Repeat the lead and test steps until the children are firm.

Questions with More Than One Answer

When presenting questions that admit to various answers (such as the second part of question 6), not all the children will be producing the same response. Permit the children to respond together. However, to make sure that individual children within the group are giving appropriate answers, call on different children after the group responds:

"Connie, how did the paint get there?" If the child answers the question reasonably well, praise the child. "Good answering, Connie."

If not, read the relevant sentences to the group. "Listen: I'll read the part of the story that answers that question."

After reading the part of the story, present the question again.

Call on at least three children to answer these questions.

Picture Comprehension
(Stories 1–160)

The last exercise dealing with the story on each lesson is picture comprehension. For this task, the children refer to the story picture and answer questions that are based on the content of the story and the details that are present in the picture.

The illustrations to some stories appear on the same page as the text. For other stories, the picture is on the next page. When the picture is on the next page the comprehension activities involve prediction questions that require the children to tell what they think they will see in the picture. For stories in which the picture is on the same page as the text, prediction questions do not appear.

EXERCISE 15

Picture comprehension

a. What do you think you'll see in the picture? (The children respond.)
b. Turn the page and look at the picture.
c. (Ask these questions:)
  1. What is that little dog doing? (Signal.) *Painting her nose.*
  2. What is behind that little dog's ear? (Signal.) *A paintbrush.* Yes, another paintbrush.
  3. Did you ever paint your nose? (The children respond.)
  4. What do you like to paint best? (Let the children comment for ten seconds. Then comment briefly.)

Lesson 2

Critical Behaviors

The questions in the picture comprehension activities are designed to allow the children to express themselves. But you must draw a line between letting the children elaborate about things that are important to them and keeping the lesson moving.

1. A good procedure is to present the questions to the group, allowing more than one child to talk at the same time. Then call on individual children to respond.

2. If you find it difficult to allow all the children to respond when they are giving different answers, simply call on different children.

3. Do not allow wrong answers. If the children have trouble identifying some of the things that are illustrated, tell them what you think they are. Also accept responses that are different from the ones you would give but that seem acceptable.

Story Reading Format from Lesson 23
(Questions on First and Second Readings)

In lesson 19, a story-reading format is introduced in which questions are presented to the children on both the first and second reading of the story. The sample format is for story 23.

Two types of items are introduced on the *first* reading:

1. Questions that ask about what a character in the story said.

2. Items that relate to directions that are given to the reader. For example, the story tells the reader, "Tell Spot what the man said." (Question 7.) This is a direction which calls for a reader response.

- The procedures for handling the first-reading items are the same as those outlined on page 33 (Critical Behaviors for Exercise 12).

The items that are to be presented on the first reading are listed under exercise 13. Notice that in the first reading not every sentence that is underlined in the boxed story has a related item. You may find it useful to underline the sentences of the boxed story in your *Presentation Book.* Use two colors, one for first-reading items, another for items that appear on both first and second readings. For example, underline all the sentences that involve first-reading items in red; underline all sentences that have both first- and second-reading items in blue. The underlined sentences that remain black are to be presented on the second reading only.

- The two basic story-reading procedures are in effect through Blocks One and Two. See page 73 for the procedures for Block Three.

EXERCISE 13

First reading—title and three sentences

a. Look at the story on page 48.
b. Everybody, touch the title of the story and get ready to read it the fast way.
c. Get ready. (Tap.) *Spot.*
d. Everybody, say the title. (Signal.) *Spot.*
e. Everybody, get ready to read this story the fast way.
f. First word. ✔
- (Pause two seconds.) Get ready. (Tap.) *This.*
g. Next word. ✔
- (Pause two seconds.) Get ready. (Tap.) *is.*
h. (Repeat *g* for the remaining words in the first three sentences. Have the children reread the first three sentences until firm.)

> spot [1]
> this is a story of a dog
> named spot. [2] spot did not hear
> well. [3] the other day she went to
> a store to get some bones. [4] the
> man in the store said, "it is a
> fine day." [5]
> "what did you say?" spot
> asked. [6]
> tell spot what the man said. [7]
> the man got some bones for
> spot. he said, "pay me a dime
> for these bones." [8]
> spot asked, "what did you
> say?"
> tell spot what the man said. [9]
> spot did not hear the man
> and the man was getting mad at
> spot. [10] the man said, "give me a
> dime for these bones." [11]
> spot asked, "what did you
> say?"
> tell spot what the man said. [12]
> spot said, "it is time for me
> to leave. so I will pay you a
> dime for the bones and I will
> go home."
> so spot gave the man a dime. [13]
> then she took the bones home
> and had a fine meal of bones.
> the end

EXERCISE 14

Remaining sentences and questions

a. I'm going to call on individual children to read a sentence. Everybody, follow along and point to the words. If you hear a mistake, raise your hand.
b. (Call on a child.) Read the next sentence.
c. (Call on another child.) Read the next sentence.

To Correct

> **word-identification errors**
> **(from, for example)**
> 1. That word is **from.** What word? *From.*
> 2. Go back to the beginning of the sentence and read the sentence again.

d. (Repeat *c* for most of the remaining sentences in the story.)
e. (Occasionally have the group read a sentence. When the group is to read, say:) Everybody, read the next sentence. (Tap for each word in the sentence.)
f. (After each underlined sentence has been read, present each comprehension question specified below to the entire group.)
[1] What's this story going to be about? (Signal.) *Spot.*
[2] What is Spot? (Signal.) *A dog.*
[3] Did Spot hear well? (Signal.) *No.* She does not hear well. So we'll have to repeat things for Spot.
[5] What did the man say? (Signal.) *It is a fine day.*
- (Repeat the question until the children give a firm response.)
[7] Everybody, tell Spot what the man said. (Signal.) *It is a fine day.*
[8] Everybody, what did the man say now? (Signal.) *Pay me a dime for these bones.*
- (Repeat the question until the children give a firm response.)
[9] Everybody, tell Spot what the man said. (Signal.) *Pay me a dime for these bones.*
[11] Everybody, what did the man say? (Signal.) *Give me a dime for these bones.*
- (Repeat the question until the children give a firm response.)
[12] Everybody, tell Spot what the man said. (Signal.) *Give me a dime for these bones.*

EXERCISE 15

Second reading—sentences and questions

a. You're going to read the story again. And I'm going to ask more questions.
b. Starting with the first word of the title. ✔
- Get ready. (Tap as the children read the title.)
c. (Call on a child.) Read the first sentence.
d. (Call on another child.) Read the next sentence.
e. (Repeat *d* for most of the remaining sentences in the story.)
f. (Occasionally have the group read a sentence.)
g. (After each underlined sentence has been read, present each comprehension question specified below to the entire group.)
[4] Why did she go to the store? (Signal.) *To get some bones.*
[6] What did Spot ask? (Signal.) *What did you say?*
- Why did Spot ask that? (The children respond.)
[10] Why do you think the man was getting mad at Spot? (The children respond.)
[13] How much did Spot pay for the bones? (Signal.) *A dime.*

EXERCISE 16

Picture comprehension

a. Look at the picture.
b. (Ask these questions:)
1. Why do you think Spot has her paw on her ear like that? (Let the children comment for ten seconds. Then comment briefly.)
2. What is Spot carrying? (Signal.) *Bones.*
3. What do you think that man is saying? (The children respond.)
4. What do you think Spot wants to do with those bones? (The children respond.)

Lesson 23

Individual Fluency Checkouts: Rate/Accuracy

Fluency Checkouts appear in lessons 5, 10, 15, and every fifth lesson until the end of the program. The Fluency Checkouts are presented to the children individually. They provide the children with practice in reading a long passage aloud. (In the group, children often do not receive this practice.) The Fluency Checkouts also demonstrate to the children that they are to use the strategy of reading the fast way and are not to continue sounding out words.

For you, the Fluency Checkouts provide information about the children's progress. (This information does not duplicate the information from the Reading Accuracy Tests, which do not measure rate.)

To pass a Fluency Checkout, a child must read a selection within a specified period of time. The maximum number of errors and the time vary from Fluency Checkout to Fluency Checkout, but these details are specified in the Fluency Checkout instructions.

Below is a Fluency Checkout from lesson 5. It describes the Fluency Checkout procedure.

★ INDIVIDUAL CHECKOUT
EXERCISE 19

2½-minute individual fluency checkout: rate/accuracy

(Make a permanent chart with children's names and lesson numbers. See the Teacher's Guide for a sample chart.)

a. As you are doing your worksheet, I'll call on children one at a time to read the **whole story**. If you can read the whole story in less than two and a half minutes, and if you make no more than three errors, I'll put two stars after your name on the chart for lesson 5.

b. If you make too many errors or don't read in less than two and a half minutes, you'll have to practice and do it again. When you do read it in under two and a half minutes with no more than three errors, you'll get one star. Remember, two stars if you can do it the first time, one star if you do it the second or third time you try.

c. (Call on each child. Tell the child:) Start with the title and read the whole story carefully. Go. (Time the child. If the child makes a mistake, quickly tell the child the correct word and permit the child to continue reading. As soon as the child makes the fourth error or exceeds the time limit, tell the child to stop.) You'll have to read the story to yourself and try again later. (Plan to monitor the child's practice.)

d. (Record two stars for each child who reads appropriately. Congratulate those children.)

e. (Give children who do not earn two stars a chance to read the story again before the next lesson is presented. Award one star to each of those children who meet the rate and accuracy criterion.)

113 words/**2.5 min** = 45 wpm **[3 errors]**

Lesson 5

The Fluency Checkout for lesson 5 directs the child to read the whole story (113 words) in no more than two and a half minutes with a maximum of three errors. (The child's rate would be at least forty-five words per minute.) Instructions for Fluency Checkouts specify what part of the story the child should read, in how many minutes, and the maximum number of acceptable errors (ranging from three to five). The last three Fluency Checkouts for the program (lessons 150, 155, and 160) specify a selection of about 180 words to be read in two minutes with a maximum of five errors. This reading rate would be ninety words per minute.

Firming

If more than one-third of the children in the group fail to pass the third Fluency Checkout (lesson 15 for groups that enter the program at lesson 1; lesson 25 for groups that enter the program at lesson 11), you should carefully examine your teaching procedures because the children are not performing acceptably. Pay particular attention to the way you present all reading vocabulary tasks, and make sure that you are presenting a sufficient number of individual turns (reading a column of words) to the lower performers in the group. Also, consider placing the children who do not pass the Fluency Checkouts on the first trial in a group that is reading an earlier lesson in the program.

If children make more than the maximum number of errors specified and do not complete the Fluency Checkout selection in the specified time, do *not* work on reading rate. Work on accuracy, and do not encourage the children to try to read fast. Simply give them a lot more practice at reading accurately. As their accuracy improves, praise them when they read faster, but make it very clear that they are to read accurately.

If children make many errors because they are trying to read fast, tell them to slow down. The rates that are specified for the Fluency Checkouts are easily mastered by the children without rushing. Remember, the priority is accuracy first; rate will follow with practice and reinforcement.

Some teachers prepare children for Fluency Checkouts by directing the children to read to another child in the class or to practice reading silently before the Fluency Checkout.

Sometimes you may be unable to complete the Fluency Checkout during one lesson. If all Fluency Checkouts are not completed, finish the Fluency Checkouts on the following day.

Chart

The Individual Fluency Checkout Chart is on page 111 of this guide. It may be reproduced for use in your classroom. Below is a sample from the chart. Two stars indicate that Ruiz read the story on the first trial in under two and a half minutes with no more than three errors. Lin's star was awarded on the second or third trial.

Sample Individual Checkout Chart

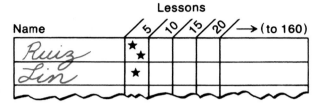

READ THE ITEMS FOR BLOCK ONE

The track begins in lesson 3 and continues through lesson 111. The track contains three formats, all of which appear in Block One.

Read-the-items exercises are designed to teach comprehension skills and to give the teacher a test of whether the children are extracting the appropriate information from what they read. The items that the children read are not predictable and must therefore be read carefully. Read-the-Items exercise appear in lessons 3 through 9 and 13 through 39. The exercises occur in the lesson after the reading vocabulary and before the story reading. The items appear in the reader. Shown here are the teacher presentation and the student material for the first read-the-items exercise.

---

rēad the Items

1. when the tēacher says "gō," stand up.

2. when the tēacher says "gō," clap.

Lesson 3 Storybook

STORYBOOK

★ READ THE ITEMS 3

EXERCISE 2

Read items 1 and 2

a. (Pass out Storybook 1.)

b. Open your reader to page 5. Get ready to read the items.

c. Finger under the first word of item 1. ✔

d. First word. (Pause.) Get ready. (Tap.) *When.*

e. Next word. (Pause.) Get ready. (Tap.) *The.*

f. (Repeat *e* for the remaining words in item 1.)

g. (Repeat *c* through *f* until item 1 is firm.)

h. Everybody, say item 1. (Pause. Signal.) *When the teacher says "Go," stand up.*

To Correct
1. Everybody, say the item with me. (Signal. Say the item with the children at a normal speaking rate.)
• (Repeat until firm.)
2. (Repeat *h*. Then skip to *j*.)

i. Again. (Repeat *h* until firm.)

j. What are you going to do when I say "**Go**"? (Signal.) *Stand up.*

• When are you going to **stand up**? (Signal.) *When the teacher says "Go."*

To Correct
(Have the children read the item aloud. Then repeat the questions.)

k. Finger under the first word of item 2. ✔

l. (Repeat *d* through *j* for item 2: When the teacher says "Go," clap.)

EXERCISE 3

Play the game with items 1 and 2

a. Read item 1 to yourself and think about what you're going to do and when you're going to do it. Raise your hand when you're ready. ✔

b. (After the children raise their hands, say:) Get ready to play the game.

c. My turn. (Pause.) Go. (Signal.) (The children are to stand up immediately.)

To Correct
(Have the children read the item aloud. Then play the game again.)

d. (Repeat *a* through *c* for item 2.)

Lesson 3 Presentation Book

Read-the-items Format

In exercise 2, the children read items 1 and 2 and answer comprehension questions. In exercise 3, the children apply each item to a game situation.

Critical Behaviors for Exercise 2
(Read Items 1 and 2)

1. In steps *c* through *g* of exercise 2, the children read the first item, one word at a time. *(When the teacher says "Go," stand up.)*

2. In step *h*, the children say item one.
   - Children are to say the item in a normal speaking rate. They are not to say the item as if they are reading it.
   - Children are to pause between the two parts of the sentence. *(When the teacher says "Go,"* (pause) *stand up.)* The pause will help the children answer comprehension questions.

3. In step *j*, after the sentence saying is firm, you present the first comprehension question: "What are you going to do when I say 'Go'?"
   - Use a hand signal to present this task. Hold your hand out as if you are stopping traffic when you ask the question. Do not move your hand until after you have completed the question.
   - After the last word of the question, pause the standard interval. Then drop your hand. Children are to respond when your hand drops.
     (If you wish, you can substitute a finger snap or a foot stamp for the hand-drop signal. In all cases, however, the timing must be the same as in other signal tasks.)
   - In step *j*, you also ask the second question about item 1: "When are you going to stand up?" Use the same signaling procedure outlined above for the first question.

Note: If the children are dealing with a difficult item, you can make their task of answering questions easier by holding the last word in the question, thereby giving the children more thinking time:
   "What are you going to do when I say 'Gooooooo'?"

Remember, the same signal-interval must be used in all signaling tasks. That interval is the time from the end of what you say until your hand drops.

4. In step *l* of the format, substitute the appropriate questions for the second item. The second item is: *When the teacher says "Go," clap.*
   - The first question you ask is: "What are you going to do when I say 'Go'?"
   - The second question is: "When are you going to clap?"

Note that these questions are not specified in the format for the second item. The rule is this: The first question for an item always begins, "What are you going to do when I. . .?"

The second question always begins, "When are you going to. . .?"

PRACTICE: Test yourself on these items.

1. *When the teacher stands up, say "Go".* What's the first question?

   What are you going to do when I stand up?

   What's the second question?
   When are you going to say "Go"?

2. *When the teacher says "Clap," touch your head.*
   What's the first question?

   What are you going to do when I say "Clap"?

   What's the second question?
   When are you going to touch your head?

3. *When the teacher holds up a hand, touch the floor.*
   What's the first question?

   What are you going to do when I hold up a hand?

   What's the second question?
   When are you going to touch the floor?

Before presenting any read-the-items tasks, read the items and make sure that you can present both questions that you will ask the children.

Critical Behaviors for Exercise 3
(Playing the Game)

After the children have read both items until firm and have answered the two comprehension questions for each item, they go to exercise 3 and play the game. For this exercise, the children read the item to themselves. Then the teacher performs the action described in the first part of the rule. The children respond by doing what the second part of the rule tells them to do.

- In step *a,* the children read item 1 to themselves *(When the teacher says "Go," stand up).* Children are to raise their hands when they have read the item.

1. Unless the children are quite fluent in reading, require them to touch under each of the words they read.

2. Do not require the children to read without moving their lips or without actually saying the words. Reading silently is often difficult for young children. If you wish, insist that they whisper when they read the items to themselves (rather than reading in a loud voice).

EXERCISE 3

Play the game with items 1 and 2

a. Read item 1 to yourself and think about what you're going to do and when you're going to do it. Raise your hand when you're ready. ✔

b. (After the children raise their hands, say:) Get ready to play the game.

c. My turn. (Pause.) Go. (Signal.) (The children are to stand up immediately.)

To Correct
(Have the children read the item aloud. Then play the game again.)

d. (Repeat *a* through *c* for item 2.)

Lesson 3

---

3. Watch the children as they read. Watch the words they are touching and what they are saying to themselves.

4. When the children raise their hands, acknowledge that you have noticed them. "Okay, Zig . . . Good, Elaine." Do not require children to keep their hands raised.

5. After children have raised their hands, ask some of them, "Do you know what you're going to do and when you're going to do it?" (Practice this question. It helps give the children a way of testing themselves as they read the item.)

- In step *b,* after the children have read the item, you tell them, "Get ready to play the game."

- In step *c,* they play the game.

1. Say "My turn." Hold out your hand as if stopping traffic.

2. Pause. Then say "Go." Signal by dropping your hand. Children are to stand up as your hand drops. They are not to wait for other children to stand up.

- You repeat steps *a* through *c* of the format for item 2. *(When the teacher says "Go," clap.)*

  When playing the game for this item, what do you do?

  Say "Go."

  What do the children do?

  Clap

PRACTICE: Let's say you present these items:

1. *When the teacher says "Clap," touch your head.*
   What do you do?

   Say "Clap."

   What do the children do?

   Touch their head

2. *When the teacher holds up a hand, touch the floor.*
   What do you do?

   Hold up a hand.

   What do the children do?

   Touch the floor.

Corrections for Exercise 2

(Read Items 1 and 2)

The children may make reading mistakes, sentence-saying mistakes, and comprehension mistakes.

- Anticipate the following types of reading mistakes in steps c through g, particularly with lower-performing groups:

  Children omit word endings: calling hands "hand."

  Children confuse words *says* and *say.*

  Children confuse words *you* and *your.*

  Children anticipate the next word in the sentence and misread the word.

Correction for Reading Mistakes

1. As soon as you hear an error, say the correct word.

2. Then direct the children to "Sound it out." Use the "Get ready" and the tapping signals specified on page 33.

- In step h, the children may make a variety of sentence-saying mistakes.

  They may omit words.

  They may add words.

  They may not say the sentence at a normal speaking rate and with appropriate pause between the two parts.

Correction for Sentence-Saying Mistakes

Correct sentence-saying mistakes by using a *lead-test* procedure (specified in the format).

1. *Lead:* Say the item with me. (Signal). When the teacher says "Go," (pause) stand up.

2. Repeat the lead step until the children are saying every word with you and pausing appropriately between the parts of the sentence. With less proficient children, you may have to repeat the lead as many as ten or more times. If the children have serious trouble saying the sentence as you lead them, encourage them. That was better. Let's say it again. (Signal).

3. *Test* the children: Your turn. Say item one. (Signal).

Corrections for Comprehension Mistakes

Children may make a variety of comprehension mistakes when asked what they are going to do (step j) and when they are going to do the action (step j).

Correct mistakes by following the correction specified in the format.

1. Have the children read the item aloud. (A good idea is to tap for each word without saying "Get ready" and "Next word." Read with the children so that they can "hear" what the entire item says.)

2. After children have read the item, repeat the question they missed.

- If children fail to respond, have them say the item. Then repeat the question.

- For extremely less proficient children rephrase the questions:

  When the teacher says "Go," what are you going to do? The children respond: *stand up.*

  You're going to stand up. When are you going to do that? The children respond: *when the teacher says "Go."*

  Repeat both questions until the children are firm.

Corrections for Exercise 3

(Playing the Game)

If children do not perform the action called for in Exercise 3 after you do your action, use the correction procedure specified on the page.

1. Have the children read the item aloud. (Read the item with them and tap for each word without saying "Get ready" or "Next word.")

2. Then present step b: Get ready to play the game . . . . Continue with step c.

- If children are less proficient in language skills, use this correction:

1. As soon as you note that the children did not respond appropriately, ask: What did I just say? Children respond *go.*

2. What are you supposed to do when the teacher says "Go?" Children respond *stand up.*

3. Remember that. Let's play the game again. My turn. Present step c.

Read-the-Items "Fooler" Format

Beginning in lesson 26, a variation of read the items is introduced in which "foolers" occur. A "fooler" is a game situation in which the teacher performs the wrong action. The children are not to respond. The fooler is presented after the children have read the items, said the items, and answered the comprehension questions. The purpose of the foolers is to teach the children how to apply a "rule" appropriately. The "fooler" format from lesson 26 is shown in exercise 11 of the example.

Critical Behaviors for Exercise 10
(Preparation for the game)

1. In step *e,* the children say the item *(When the teacher stands up, say "Stand up").*

2. In step *f,* the teacher asks, "What are you going to say when I stand up?" The children respond, "Stand up."

3. In step *g,* the teacher asks, "What are you going to say when I touch my ear?" The children respond, "Nothing."

4. In steps *h* and *i,* the teacher asks two more similar questions that help firm the children on what they are going to do.

    Perhaps the most critical behavior in presenting fooler tasks is *pacing.* You move very quickly after the children say the rule (step *e* in exercise 10).

STORYBOOK

READ THE ITEM 26
EXERCISE 10

Read the item

a. (Pass out Storybook 1.)
b. Open your reader to page 57. Get ready to read the item.
c. Finger under the first word of the item. ✔
d. Get ready. (Tap. Tap for each word in item 1. Repeat until firm.)
e. Everybody, get ready to say the item. (Pause. Signal.) *When the teacher stands up, say "Stand up."*
• (Repeat until firm.)
f. What are you going to say when I stand up? (Signal.) *"Stand up."* Right.
g. What are you going to do when I touch my ear? (Signal.) *Nothing.* Right.

To Correct
1. (Give the answer.)
2. (Then have the children read the item aloud.)
3. (Repeat the question.)

h. What are you going to do when I say "**Stand up**"? (Signal.) *Nothing.* Right.
i. What are you going to say when I stand up? (Signal.) *"Stand up."*

Note: Practice this exercise before presenting it.

EXERCISE 11

Fooler game

To Correct
mistakes on foolers
1. What did I (say, do)? (Signal.)
2. Everybody, read the item out loud. First word. Get ready. (Tap for each word.)
3. Does the item tell you what to do when I (say, do _____)? (Signal.) *No.*
4. So you don't do anything. I fooled you.
5. (Repeat the fooler game.)

a. Let's play the game and see if I can fool you.
b. My turn. (Hold your hand out. Pause. Touch your ear. Pause. Drop your hand. Praise the children who do nothing.)
c. My turn. (Hold your hand out. Pause. Say:) Stand up. (Pause. Drop your hand. Praise the children who do nothing.)
d. My turn. (Hold your hand out. Pause. Stand up. Pause. Drop your hand.) (The children are to say *Stand up* immediately.)
• (Praise the children who say "Stand up.")

Lesson 26

Critical Behaviors for Exercise 11
(Fooler game with the children)

1. In exercise 11, pause before presenting each action. Aside from that pause, move quickly.

   - In step *a,* say the instructions quickly.
   - In step *b,* do not be elaborate in your praise. "Good job. I couldn't fool you. Let's keep going."
   - Move to step *c.* If you go slowly, the children will forget the item and make mistakes.

2. If the children require some firming on the questions at the end of exercise 10, repeat the item before presenting exercise 11. "Let's play the game and see if I can fool you. Remember the item: When the teacher stands up, say 'Stand up.'"

3. At this point, you may want low performers to repeat the rule several times before playing the game.

4. Also, for these low-performing children you may want to present the steps in the task with more structure.

   - For example, you would present step *b* this way: "My turn": Hold your hand out. (Pause.) Touch your ear. "Everybody, tell me what I did." (Signal.) The children respond, "You touched your ear."
   "Yes, I touched my ear. Now show me what you do when I touch my ear." (Pause.) "Get ready." (Hand-drop signal.)
   - You would present step *c* this way: "My turn." Hold your hand out. (Pause.) Say "Stand up." Say "Everybody, tell me what I said." (Signal.) The children respond, "Stand up."
   - "Yes, I said 'Stand up.' Now show me what you do when I *say* 'Stand up.'"
   If the children are low performers, practice presenting the fooler tasks in this way. When the children catch on to the format, return to the format that appears in the *Teacher Presentation Book.*

Corrections

The corrections for exercise 10 and exercise 11 are specified in the format. Follow these corrections if children make mistakes.

PRACTICE the correction in exercise 11 before working with the children. The words that go in the blank of step 3 describe a wrong action that you did. If you just said "Stand up" (a wrong action), the wording of step 3 would be: "Does the item tell you what to do when I say 'Stand up?'"

If you just touched your ear (a wrong action), the wording of step 3 would be: "Does the item tell you what to do when I touch my ear?"

Use this correction when the children respond to any wrong action that you perform in the fooler game.

WORKSHEETS FOR BLOCK ONE

Worksheets begin in lesson 1 and continue through lesson 160. Worksheet activities are presented as the last part of the daily lesson.

The Worksheets provide a very important component of the program. They teach the children important "test-taking skills." They reinforce reading skills that have been taught in the daily lessons. They expand the children's reading skills through exercises that require independent work.

To make the Worksheet program effective, you must do more than circle errors on children's papers. You must care about the mistakes, correct them, let the children know that you are attending to the performance on Worksheet activities, and reinforce children for making few or no errors on the Worksheet.

Two types of Worksheet activities are presented.

1. Written exercises that are directed by the teacher and specified in the *Teacher Presentation Book.*

2. Written exercises that are done independently by the children in a 20–30 minute period, which does not have to follow the reading period and may be scheduled at another time during the day.

Six different Worksheet exercises appear in Block One. Below is a list of the exercises and the lessons in which they appear:

Story Items	Lessons 1–160
Sound Writing	Lessons 1–25
Picture Comprehension	Lessons 1–25
Sentence Copying	Lessons 3–48
Reading Comprehension	Lessons 8–160
Following Instructions Type 1	Lessons 18–46

Story Items (Lesson 2)

The first activity on the Worksheets for Block One is titled *Story Items.* These are comprehension items that refer to the story the children have just read. The story-items exercises in Block One involve circling the appropriate word to complete the item. The teacher-directed formats appear in lessons 1, 2, 5, 6, 7, 10, 11, and 12. After lesson 12 the children do the story items independently.

The instructions from the Presentation Book and the story items for lesson 2 are shown here.

Note that the large heading at the top of the teacher presentation page indicates that story items and the activities that follow involve Worksheet 2.

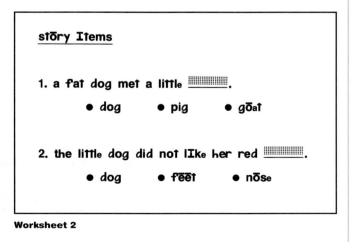

Worksheet 2

WORKSHEET 2

STORY ITEMS

The children will need pencils.

EXERCISE 16

Read and complete story items

a. (Pass out Worksheet 2 to each child.)

b. (Hold up side 1 of your worksheet and point to the story items exercise.) Everybody, these items are about the story you just read.

c. (Point to the blank in item 1.) Something is missing. When you get to this blank, say "**blank.**" What will you say? (Signal.) *Blank.*

d. Get ready to read item 1 the fast way. First word. ✔
• Get ready. (Tap.) *A.*

e. Next word. ✔
• Get ready. (Tap.) *Fat.*

f. (Repeat e for the remaining words in item 1.)

g. (Repeat d through f until firm.)

h. The story said that a fat dog met a little … something. Everybody, what did the fat dog meet? (Signal.) *A little dog.*

i. (Repeat h until firm.)

j. Everybody, get ready to touch the word under item 1 that tells what the fat dog met. (Pause.) Get ready. (Signal.) ✔

k. Circle that word. ✔

l. Everybody, touch item 2. ✔
• Get ready to read item 2 the fast way. First word. ✔
• Get ready. (Tap.) *The.*

m. Next word. ✔
• Get ready. (Tap.) *Little.*

n. (Repeat m for the remaining words in item 2.)

o. The little dog did not like her red . . . something. Everybody, what was that red something the little dog did not like? (Signal.) *Her nose.*

p. (Repeat o until firm.)

q. Everybody, get ready to touch the word under item 2 that tells what red something the little dog did not like. (Pause.) Get ready. (Signal.) ✔

r. Circle that word. ✔

Lesson 2

Critical Behaviors

1. In steps *d* through *f*, the children read item 1: *A fat dog met a little blank.*
2. In step *j*, the children touch the word under item 1 that tells what the fat dog met. Children are not to touch the word until you signal.
3. In step *k*, the children circle the word.
4. Follow the signaling procedures specified for other teacher presentation tasks.

   Note that the blanks for story items 1 and 2 on the Worksheet are designed so that children will not write in them.

Story Items (Lesson 10)

The second teacher-directed story-items format is introduced in lesson 10 and appears in lessons 10, 11, and 12.

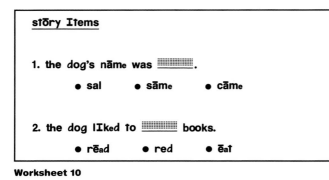

WORKSHEET 10
STORY ITEMS
EXERCISE 15
Read story items

a. (Pass out Worksheet 10 to each child.)
b. (Hold up side 1 of your worksheet. Point to the words **story items**.)
   Everybody, you're going to read the items for the story you just read. You're going to write the answers later.
c. Get ready to read item 1 the fast way. First word. ✔
 • Get ready. (Tap.) *The.*
d. Next word. ✔
 • Get ready. (Tap.) *Dog's.*
e. (Repeat *d* for the remaining words in item 1.)
f. Tell me the answer. The dog's name was blank. What goes in the blank? (Pause. Signal.) *Sal.* (The children are not to circle the answers now.)
g. (Repeat *c* through *f* for item 2.)
h. You're going to do these items later. Remember to circle the right answer for each item.

Lesson 10

story Items

1. the dog's nāme was ▨▨▨▨▨.
   • sal   • sāme   • cāme

2. the dog līked to ▨▨▨▨▨ books.
   • rēad   • red   • ēat

Worksheet 10

This format is different from the introductory format in several ways.

1. The children circle the appropriate response later, not as part of the teacher-directed work.

2. The procedures for the second item are not specified. The teacher is directed to adapt steps *c* through *f* to the second item.

   Beginning in lesson 14, the story-item work is no longer teacher-directed. A "tag" like the one below appears in the daily teacher-presentation lesson. It tells the children to work the items independently.

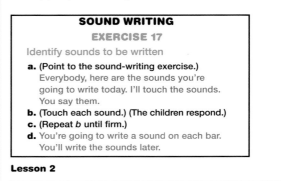

Story items
(Point to the story items exercise.) Here are the items about the story you just read. Read the items and circle the answers that tell what happened in the story.

Lesson 14

Sound Writing

The Sound Writing track begins in lesson 1 and continues through lesson 25. The sound writing section of the Worksheet displays a model sound on the left of each line. The children are to copy that sound on each empty block on the line. A light dotted line helps the children make the small and tall letters the appropriate height.

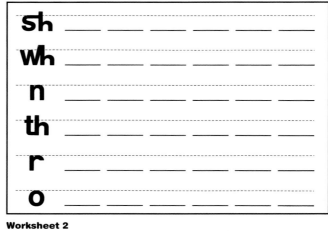

SOUND WRITING
EXERCISE 17
Identify sounds to be written

a. (Point to the sound-writing exercise.)
   Everybody, here are the sounds you're going to write today. I'll touch the sounds. You say them.
b. (Touch each sound.) (The children respond.)
c. (Repeat *b* until firm.)
d. You're going to write a sound on each bar. You'll write the sounds later.

Lesson 2

Worksheet 2

The teacher-directed format shown below is taken from lesson 2. The format appears in lessons 1, 2, 3, 4, 11, and 12. On remaining days, the children work independently.

Picture Comprehension (Lesson 1)

The Picture Comprehension track begins in lesson 1 and continues through lesson 25. Teacher-directed presentation occurs in lessons 1 through 4, 11, and 12. "Tags" that direct the children to work independently appear in other lessons.

Here is the teacher presentation and the student Worksheet from lesson 2.

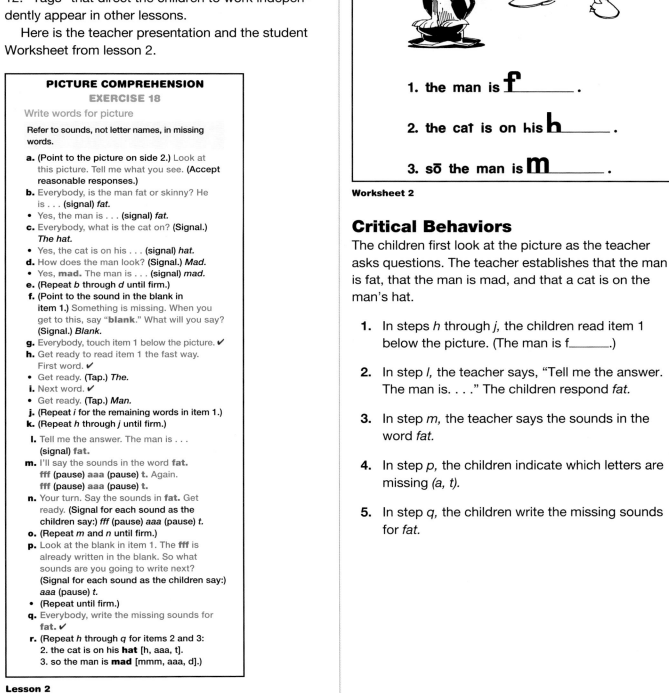

Worksheet 2

PICTURE COMPREHENSION
EXERCISE 18

Write words for picture

Refer to sounds, not letter names, in missing words.

a. (Point to the picture on side 2.) Look at this picture. Tell me what you see. **(Accept reasonable responses.)**

b. Everybody, is the man fat or skinny? He is . . . (signal) *fat.*
• Yes, the man is . . . (signal) *fat.*

c. Everybody, what is the cat on? (Signal.) *The hat.*
• Yes, the cat is on his . . . (signal) *hat.*

d. How does the man look? (Signal.) *Mad.*
• Yes, **mad.** The man is . . . (signal) *mad.*

e. (Repeat *b* through *d* until firm.)

f. (Point to the sound in the blank in item 1.) Something is missing. When you get to this, say "**blank.**" What will you say? (Signal.) *Blank.*

g. Everybody, touch item 1 below the picture. ✔

h. Get ready to read item 1 the fast way. First word. ✔
• Get ready. (Tap.) *The.*

i. Next word. ✔
• Get ready. (Tap.) *Man.*

j. (Repeat *i* for the remaining words in item 1.)

k. (Repeat *h* through *j* until firm.)

l. Tell me the answer. The man is . . . (signal) **fat.**

m. I'll say the sounds in the word **fat.**
fff (pause) **aaa** (pause) **t.** Again.
fff (pause) **aaa** (pause) **t.**

n. Your turn. Say the sounds in **fat.** Get ready. (Signal for each sound as the children say:) **fff** (pause) **aaa** (pause) **t.**

o. (Repeat *m* and *n* until firm.)

p. Look at the blank in item 1. The **fff** is already written in the blank. So what sounds are you going to write next? (Signal for each sound as the children say:) **aaa** (pause) **t.**
• (Repeat until firm.)

q. Everybody, write the missing sounds for **fat.** ✔

r. (Repeat *h* through *q* for items 2 and 3:
2. the cat is on his **hat** [h, aaa, t].
3. so the man is **mad** [mmm, aaa, d].)

Lesson 2

Critical Behaviors

The children first look at the picture as the teacher asks questions. The teacher establishes that the man is fat, that the man is mad, and that a cat is on the man's hat.

1. In steps *h* through *j*, the children read item 1 below the picture. (The man is f_____.)

2. In step *l*, the teacher says, "Tell me the answer. The man is. . . ." The children respond *fat.*

3. In step *m*, the teacher says the sounds in the word *fat.*

4. In step *p*, the children indicate which letters are missing *(a, t).*

5. In step *q*, the children write the missing sounds for *fat.*

Corrections

Children may have trouble in steps *l, p,* and *q.*

To correct mistakes in step *l,* prompt the children by saying the first sound that appears in the blank. Tell me the answer. The man is (pause) **fffff**. . . . . Signal.

In step *p,* the children may not respond appropriately. If they have trouble, use this correction:

1. Let's say the sounds for **fat.** Get ready. **Fffaaat.**

2. Let's do it again. This time I'll say **fff.** You say **aaa** (pause) **t.** My turn: **fff.** Your turn. (Signal.) *The children say aaa* (pause) *t.*

3. Repeat step 2 until firm.

4. Return to step *p* in the format. Look at the blank in item 1. The **fff** is already written in the blank. So what sounds are you going to write next? (Signal.) *The children say aaa* (pause) *t.*

5. Repeat step 4 until firm.

6. Quickly move to step *q.* Everybody, write the missing sounds for **fat.** Check the children's work.

In lessons 5 through 10 and 13 through 25 the children are instructed to work independently. The "tag" that appears in the daily teacher presentation material is shown below.

> Picture comprehension
> **a.** (Point to the picture.)
> Everybody, you're going to look at this picture. Then you're going to read each item and write the missing words.
> **b.** Remember—the first sound of each missing word is already written in the blank.

Lesson 21

Sentence Copying (Lesson 3)

The Sentence Copying track begins in lesson 3 and continues through lesson 48. Teacher-directed presentations occur in lessons 3, 4, 11, and 12. In other lessons, the children work independently.

In the early lessons, the Worksheet work consists of a model sentence, one dotted sentence below the model sentence, and several blank lines. The children trace the letters in the dotted sentence. They form letters by starting with the big ball. They follow the dotted line to the end. Then they go to the smaller ball and trace that line to the end.

Shown in the next column is the sentence-copying material for Lesson 3.

Note that all letters are full-sized in the sentence-copying activities. The boldface model shows a small *i* in *paint.* The sentence to be traced, however, has a full-sized *i.*

Note also that long lines appear above long-vowel letters in the sentence to be traced.

It is not critical for children to copy the long lines when they write the sentence on the lines below the sentence to be traced. It is important, however, that all letters are full-sized.

> ★ **SENTENCE COPYING**
> **EXERCISE 8**
> Read sentence to copy
> **a.** (Point to the sentence **hē had a pāint can.**)
> **b.** Here's the sentence you're going to write on the lines below.
> Everybody, touch this sentence on your worksheet. ✔
> **c.** Get ready to read the words in this sentence the fast way. First word. ✔
> • Get ready. (Tap for each word as the children read *he had a paint can.*)
> **d.** (Have the children reread the sentence the fast way.)
> **e.** (Point to the dotted words on the first line.)
> Later, you're going to trace the dotted words in this sentence. Then you're going to write those words on the other lines.

Lesson 3

> hē had a pāint can.
> hē had a pāint can.

Worksheet 3

Reading Comprehension (Lesson 8)

The Reading Comprehension track begins in lesson 8 and continues through lesson 160. The reading-comprehension exercises consist of several sentences below which are items about the content of the sentences. In Block One, the children complete the items by circling the appropriate word for each item. The vocabulary for Block One is "safe" in the sense that all words were taught earlier in the program. (Most are taken from *Reading Mastery,* Grade K vocabulary.)

Initially, the blank in each item occurs only at the end of the sentence and involves only a single word. Later, the blank occurs in the middle of the sentence (a harder task) and may involve a response that contains more than one word. The children read several sentences in the first reading-comprehension exercises. By the end of Block One, the children read two stories, about twenty-five words each.

Shown below are the teacher presentation format and the Worksheet exercise for lesson 8. Note that the exercise is labeled "reading" on the student material from lesson 8 to lesson 13.

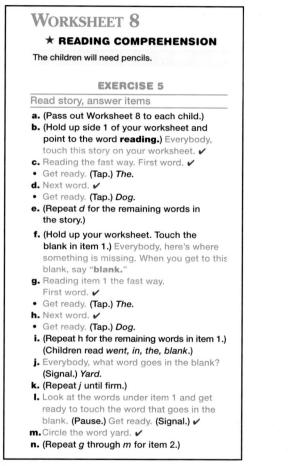

WORKSHEET 8

★ **READING COMPREHENSION**

The children will need pencils.

EXERCISE 5

Read story, answer items

a. (Pass out Worksheet 8 to each child.)
b. (Hold up side 1 of your worksheet and point to the word **reading**.) Everybody, touch this story on your worksheet. ✔
c. Reading the fast way. First word. ✔
• Get ready. (Tap.) *The.*
d. Next word. ✔
• Get ready. (Tap.) *Dog.*
e. (Repeat *d* for the remaining words in the story.)
f. (Hold up your worksheet. Touch the blank in item 1.) Everybody, here's where something is missing. When you get to this blank, say "**blank.**"
g. Reading item 1 the fast way. First word. ✔
• Get ready. (Tap.) *The.*
h. Next word. ✔
• Get ready. (Tap.) *Dog.*
i. (Repeat *h* for the remaining words in item 1.) (Children read *went, in, the, blank.*)
j. Everybody, what word goes in the blank? (Signal.) *Yard.*
k. (Repeat *j* until firm.)
l. Look at the words under item 1 and get ready to touch the word that goes in the blank. (Pause.) Get ready. (Signal.) ✔
m. Circle the word yard. ✔
n. (Repeat *g* through *m* for item 2.)

Lesson 8

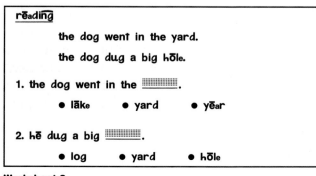

rēadĭng

the dog wenт in the yard.

the dog dug a big hōle.

1. the dog wenт in the ▓▓▓▓▓.
   • lāke   • yard   • yēar

2. hē dug a big ▓▓▓▓▓.
   • log   • yard   • hōle

Critical Behaviors

• In steps *c* through *e,* the children read both sentences until the reading is firm. The procedures are the same as those for other sentence-reading activities.
• In steps *g* through *i,* the children read item 1 below the sentences.
• In step *j,* the children identify the word that goes in the blank.
• In step *m,* the children circle the word that goes in the blank.

Corrections

If children have trouble identifying the word that goes in the blank (step *l*), correct in the following way.

1. Say: One of the sentences above the item tells where the dog **went.** Look for the word <u>went</u> and touch the sentence that tells you where he went. Check children's responses.

2. Everybody, read the sentence that tells where the dog went. First word. Get ready. . . .

3. After the children read the sentence, say: The dog went in the. . . . . (Signal.)

4. Return to step *g* in the format and repeat steps *g* through *l.*

If children have trouble with item 2, use the correction above. Have the children touch the sentence that tells what the dog **dug.** Say: Find the word <u>dug</u> and touch the sentence that tells what he dug. Check children's responses.

Note: By stressing the words that distinguish between the sentences (*went* and *dug*), you will be providing the children with a method for discriminating between bits of information that are similar.

Following Instructions

The Following Instructions track begins in lesson 18 and continues through lesson 120. There are two types of following-instructions exercises:

• Following Instructions Type 1 (lessons 18–46)
• Following instructions Type 2 (lessons 47–120)

The Following Instructions track is very important. The exercises are similar to those in Read the Items in that they require the children to read each instruction very carefully and then do what the instructions say. A major difference between Following Instructions and Read the

Items is that the children do the Following Instructions by themselves (after three teacher-directed introductions in lessons 18, 19, and 20).

Following Instructions Type 1
(Lesson 18)

The Following Instructions Type 1 presentation and the student material from lesson 18 are shown below.

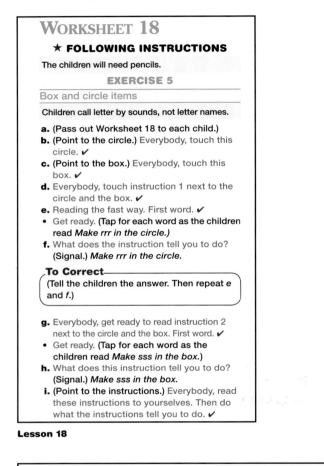

Lesson 18

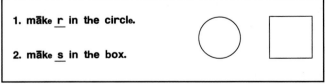

Worksheet 18

- In steps *e* through *h*, the children read both items and answer the questions presented by the teacher.
- In step *i*, the children are instructed to read the instructions to themselves, then do what the instructions tell them to do.

Critical Behaviors

1. Watch the children to make sure that they actually reread the items before responding.

2. Make sure that they do item 1 first and item 2 next.

Corrections

The most frequent problem among low performers is that they don't know prepositions, such as *in*. They may make the letters *on* the circle and box, not *in* the circle and box.

To correct:

1. Hold up Worksheet. Everybody, I'm going to touch. Tell me if I touch in the circle.

2. Touch over the circle. Is this in the circle?

3. Touch next to the circle. Is this in the circle?

4. Touch in the middle of the circle. Is this in the circle?

If children don't respond appropriately, tell them the answer and repeat the examples (in a different order) until the children are firm.
   Then:

1. Everybody, touch <u>in</u> the circle on your Worksheet. ✔

2. Everybody, touch <u>in</u> the box on your Worksheet. ✔

3. Repeat steps 2 and 3 until firm.

4. Repeat the following instructions format beginning with step *d.*

Following Instructions Type 1
(Lesson 26)

Beginning in lesson 23, the children are presented with a single object (either a box or a circle). They must discriminate between different prepositions to handle these exercises. The following Worksheet is from lesson 26.

1. mād͞e <u>m</u> in the circle.

2. mād͞e <u>a</u> ōver the circle.

3. mād͞e <u>r</u> under the circle.

Worksheet 26

Corrections

Note: If children have preposition problems, use a variation of the procedure outlined above.

First firm the children on two prepositions, *in* and *over*.

1. Hold up your Worksheet. Everybody, I'm going to touch. Tell me if I touch **in** the circle or **over** the circle.

2. Touch over the circle. Where did I touch?

3. Touch above original touch. Where did I touch?

4. Touch in the circle. Where did I touch?

5. Repeat the examples (in mixed order until the children are firm).

6. Then have them touch in the circle and over the circle on their Worksheet. Check children's responses.

7. After children are firm on *in* and *over,* introduce *under.* ("Tell me if I touch in the circle or over the circle or under the circle.")

- If children continue to make mistakes, require them to circle the word in the instruction that tells where they will make the symbol. "Item 1 tells where. Does it say *in,* or *over,* or *under?* Circle the word that tells." Check work.

   Beginning with lesson 28, items are introduced that involve a vocabulary that is less predictable than that in earlier items.

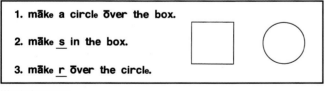

1. mā̆ke a circle ōver the box.

2. mā̆ke s in the box.

3. mā̆ke r ōver the circle.

Worksheet 36

Note that the first item involves both the words *circle* and *box.*

Critical Behaviors for Later Following Instructions

The most frequent type of errors that children make results from carelessness. They do the items quickly and often make errors. To prevent these errors, challenge the children:

- "Remember, these items are hard. They're so hard that you probably can't do all of them without making a mistake no matter how hard you try. You really have to read these instructions carefully."

- When children don't make mistakes, act somewhat surprised. "I didn't think you could do those hard, hard instructions. I don't know how you do it."

   If you set up the following-instructions tasks in this way (and follow a similar procedure for other exercises in which children tend to make mistakes), the carelessness mistakes will quickly diminish. Note that you may still have to teach the children things they don't know, particularly the meaning of prepositions to low-performing children.

Block Two

The Vowel Mechanics Block
(Lessons 40–80)

Schedule of Activities for Daily Lessons
- Vowel names (lessons 40–52)
- Reading Vocabulary words
- Story reading and teacher-directed comprehension activities
- Individual Fluency Checkouts: Rate/Accuracy
- Worksheet activities (some teacher-directed, some independent)

In Block Two the following major activities take place:

1. The children are taught the names of the vowels (*a, e, i, o, u*).

2. The children learn to discriminate between short-vowel words (*mop*) and words that have a long vowel and a full-sized final *e* (*mope*).

3. The joined letters *th, sh,* and *ing* become disjoined.

4. The children are taught to identify the sound combination *ou,* and the combinations *th, sh,* and *ing* when the letters are disjoined.

5. Story-picture items are introduced in the Worksheets.

6. Sentence-copying activities are dropped from the Worksheet activities (lesson 48).

LETTER NAMES—VOWELS
(Lessons 40–52)

The Letter Names track begins in lesson 40 and continues through lesson 52. (The track is resumed in Block Three at lesson 83 and continues through lesson 94, during which time the children are taught alphabetical order, letter names for consonants, and capital letters.) The track contains three formats.

The letter names activities are presented as the first tasks of the lesson (replacing sound-identification exercises). The introductory format that appears in lesson 40 is shown below. This format appears in two lessons.

Critical Behaviors for Exercise 1

1. Step *a* is a *model.* You touch each letter and say the name. Do not hold the name when you identify each letter. (Do not say *āāā.*) Say *ā.*

2. Step *b* is a *lead.* You touch each letter as the children say the names with you.

3. Step *e* is a *test.* You say "All by yourselves. Say the *names.*"

Critical Behaviors for Exercise 2

In exercise 2, you firm the names of two letters—*e* and *o.*

1. When presenting exercise 2, remember to give the children thinking time before you touch each letter.

2. Touch quickly, as you would touch a stop sound. The children are to respond by saying each name quickly—*ē* instead of *ēēē.*

Corrections

If children have trouble with this exercise, they are probably not firm on the preceding sounds lesson (which concentrated heavily on vowels, particularly vowels with lines over them). The best remedy might be to return to lesson 38 and repeat the sound identification exercises in lessons 38 and 39. Then present lesson 40.

Track Development

After the introduction of letter names for the vowels in lessons 40 and 41, the children receive a daily review of letter names through lesson 52. When presenting these lessons make sure that the children are firm on letter-name identification. They will use these letter-names in the Reading Vocabulary exercises.

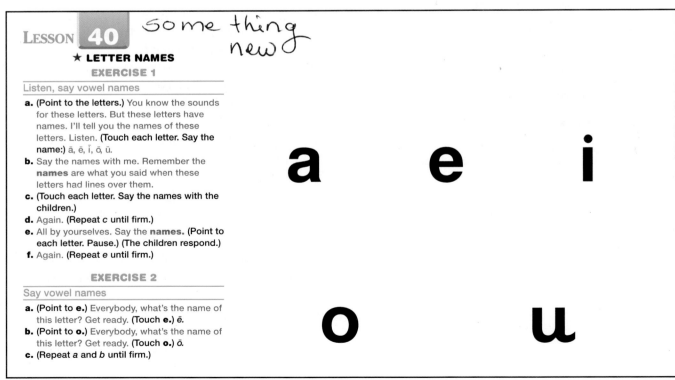

LESSON **40**   *Some thing new*

★ **LETTER NAMES**

EXERCISE 1

Listen, say vowel names

a. (Point to the letters.) You know the sounds for these letters. But these letters have names. I'll tell you the names of these letters. Listen. (Touch each letter. Say the name:) ā, ē, ī, ō, ū.
b. Say the names with me. Remember the **names** are what you said when these letters had lines over them.
c. (Touch each letter. Say the names with the children.)
d. Again. (Repeat *c* until firm.)
e. All by yourselves. Say the **names.** (Point to each letter. Pause.) (The children respond.)
f. Again. (Repeat *e* until firm.)

EXERCISE 2

Say vowel names

a. (Point to **e.**) Everybody, what's the name of this letter? Get ready. (Touch **e.**) ē.
b. (Point to **o.**) Everybody, what's the name of this letter? Get ready. (Touch **o.**) ō.
c. (Repeat *a* and *b* until firm.)

a   e   i

o   u

Lesson 40

Do not touch small letters.

Get ready to read all the words on this page without making a mistake.

EXERCISE 3

Sound out first

a. (Touch the ball for **māde.**) Sound it out. Get ready. (Quickly touch **m, ā, d** as the children say:) *mmmāāād.*
b. What word? (Signal.) *Made.* Yes, **made.**
c. (Repeat exercise until firm.)

EXERCISE 4

Sound out first

a. (Touch the ball for **mad.**) Sound it out. Get ready. (Quickly touch **m, a, d** as the children say:) *mmmaaad.*
b. What word? (Signal.) *Mad.* Yes, **mad.**
c. (Repeat exercise until firm.)

EXERCISE 5

Teach final-e rule

a. (Touch the ball for **mad.**) Everybody, read this word the fast way. Get ready. (Signal.) *Mad.* Yes, **mad.**
b. (Point to **a** in **mad.**) Here's a rule. If there is an **ē** on the end of this word, you say the **name** of this letter. Remember that rule.
c. (Point to **a** in **made.**) There's an **ē** on the end of this word. So tell me the **name** of this letter. Get ready. (Signal.) *a.* Yes, **ā.**
d. (Touch the ball for **made.**) Read this word the fast way and say the name **ā.** (Pause two seconds.) Get ready. (Signal.) *Made.*
e. What word? (Signal.) *Made.* Yes, **made.**
f. (Touch the ball for **made.**) Read the fast way. (Pause two seconds.) Get ready. (Signal.) *Mad.* Yes, **mad.**
• (Repeat until firm.)
g. (Touch the ball for **made.**) Read the fast way. (Pause two seconds.) Get ready. (Signal.) *Made.* Yes, **made.**
• (Repeat until firm.)
h. (Repeat *f* and *g* until firm.)

mad →

made

Lesson 48

READING VOCABULARY FOR BLOCK TWO

The major thrust of the Reading Vocabulary in Block Two is to teach children how to read words such as *rode* and *made* that have a final *e* and a long-vowel sound and how to discriminate between these words and regularly spelled short-vowel words (such as *mad* and *rod*).

As letter names are being taught, the children are regularly presented with Reading Vocabulary words that follow the long-e rule but that are written in Reading Mastery orthography:

This procedure strengthens identification of the words.

After letter names have been taught, the children are introduced to the rule about the final *e.* "If there is an *e* on the end of the word, you say the name of this letter" (pointing to the first vowel in the word).

Note that the rule makes reference to the *name of this letter,* which is why the vowel names are taught

before the words are introduced in the Reading Vocabulary.

The children apply the rule about the final *e* to words that are presented with no lines over the vowel and a full-sized *e.*

Teach the long-vowel-rule formats very carefully and present enough individual turns to give you feedback about how firm the children are. Beginning at lesson 76 and continuing throughout the program, children will read stories with many of the long-vowel patterns presented in Block Two. If the long-vowel exercises have not been taught well, the lower-performing children may have difficulties.

Long-Vowel-Rule Format
(Lesson 48)

The first reading-vocabulary format that deals with the long-vowel rule appears in lesson 48.

Note that the first two words on the page are repeated. In the first appearance of *made* (exercise 3), a long line and a small *e* are present. In the second appearance (exercise 5), there is no long line and the *e* is full-sized.

• In step *b* of exercise 5 (titled *Teach final-e rule*), the teacher points to the *a* in *mad* and presents the rule about the final *e:* "If there is an *ē* on the end of this word, you say the *name* of this letter."

- In step *c*, the teacher applies the rule to the word *made.* The teacher points to the *a* in *made* and tells the children, "There's an ē on the end of this word. So tell me the *name* of this letter. Get ready." (Signal.)
- In step *d*, the children read the word the fast way, saying the name *a.*
- In steps *f* and *g*, the children reread *mad* and *made* the fast way.

Critical Behaviors for Exercise 5

1. Fast pacing of the steps in this exercise is critical. In step *b*, remember to stress the word *name* in the rule. The discrimination between "the sound and the name" will be easier if you stress, ". . . You say the *name* of this letter."

PRACTICE saying the rule so that you can present it in step *b* without looking at the book. Say the rule as if it is very important. (It is.)

2. In step *c*, present the rule in parts. Pause after you say, "There's an ē on the end of this word." If you wish, you can ask the children, "Do you see it?" Or even ask one of the children to touch it.

   Then say, "So tell me the *name* of this letter. Get ready." Signal by touching just under the *a.*

Corrections for Exercise 5

- In step *a*, if the children make mistakes on reading *mad,* use the standard sound-out correction. Then repeat step *a* of the format.
- In step *c*, the children may say the sound *aaa,* not the name.

To correct:

1. Tell the children: You said the sound. I want the **name.** What's the name?

2. Repeat steps *b* and *c* of the format.

- In step *d*, some children will make mistakes when trying to say the word (particularly the first time the format is presented).

To correct:

1. Immediately tell the children the word. **Made.**

2. Relate the pronunciation to the rule. I said ā when I read the word. Listen: māāāāāde. Hear the ā?

3. Repeat steps *c* and *d* of the format until firm.

- In step *f*, children may make mistakes. They read *mad* as *made.*

To correct:

1. The correction is the standard sound-it-out, what-word correction.

2. Then repeat steps *f* and *g* until the children are quite firm on both words.

PRACTICE presenting the format and the corrections in steps *c, d,* and *f*. Work with another adult who makes the mistakes. Work on the corrections until you can execute them without referring to the format or to this guide.

Track Development

Practice Final-e Rule (Lesson 51)

Vowel-rule exercises similar to the one above are presented in lessons 48 through 50. In lesson 51, the children are introduced to a format that requires less teacher prompting. The format from lesson 52 is shown below.

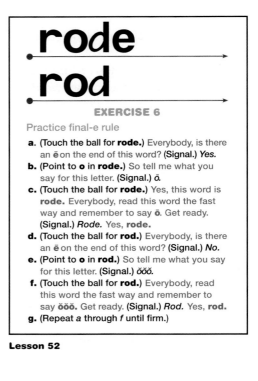

EXERCISE 6

Practice final-e rule

a. (Touch the ball for **rode.**) Everybody, is there an ē on the end of this word? (Signal.) *Yes.*
b. (Point to **o** in **rode.**) So tell me what you say for this letter. (Signal.) ō.
c. (Touch the ball for **rode.**) Yes, this word is **rode.** Everybody, read this word the fast way and remember to say ō. Get ready. (Signal.) *Rode.* Yes, **rode.**
d. (Touch the ball for **rod.**) Everybody, is there an ē on the end of this word? (Signal.) *No.*
e. (Point to **o** in **rod.**) So tell me what you say for this letter. (Signal.) ŏŏŏ.
f. (Touch the ball for **rod.**) Everybody, read this word the fast way and remember to say ŏŏŏ. Get ready. (Signal.) *Rod.* Yes, **rod.**
g. (Repeat *a* through *f* until firm.)

Lesson 52

Critical Behaviors

1. In step *c,* do not hurry the children. Pause before saying "Get ready."
   - Touch the ball for *rode.* Say "Everybody, read this word the fast way and remember to say ō." Pause for two seconds while the children figure out what they will say. If you fail to pause, some children will have trouble.
   - "Get ready." Signal by slashing right along the arrow.

2. Step *g* is critical, particularly if children made any mistakes in reading the two words. Repeat all steps—*a* through *f*—until the children can perform without making a mistake. If you follow this procedure the first time the format appears, you will discover that the children require very few corrections on subsequent vowel-rule exercises.

Corrections

- In step *a,* the children may respond weakly or incorrectly when asked, "Everybody, is there an ē on the end of the word?"

To correct step a:
1. Touch the e. Ask: What is the name of this letter? The children respond ē.

2. Ask: Where is this ē? . . . Yes, on the end of this word.

3. Repeat step *a.*
- In step *b,* the children may say the sound *ooo* in response to "So tell me what you say for this letter."

To correct step b:
1. Point to *o* and say: If there is an ē on the end of this word, you say the **name** of this letter. What's the name of this letter? The children respond ō. Yes, **ō.**

2. Repeat steps *a* and *b.*
- In step *c,* the children may say *rod.*

To correct step c:
1. Immediately tell the children the word. Rode.

2. Repeat steps *b* and *c* until firm.
- In step *e,* the children may say the name ō instead of the sound *ooo* when asked about what they say for the letter.

To correct step e:
1. Say the correct sound immediately. **ooo.**

2. Repeat step *e.*

3. Repeat steps *a* and *b, d* and *e* until the children are firm on all steps.

PRACTICE the above corrections for steps *a, b, c,* and *e.* They are very important.

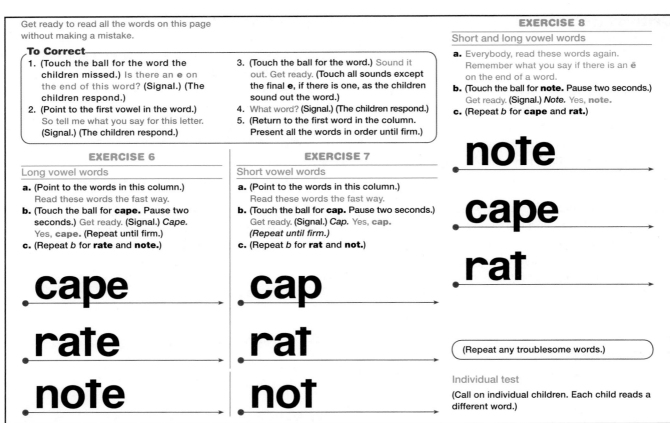

Get ready to read all the words on this page without making a mistake.

To Correct

1. (Touch the ball for the word the children missed.) Is there an **e** on the end of this word? (Signal.) (The children respond.)
2. (Point to the first vowel in the word.) So tell me what you say for this letter. (Signal.) (The children respond.)
3. (Touch the ball for the word.) Sound it out. Get ready. (Touch all sounds except the final **e**, if there is one, as the children sound out the word.)
4. What word? (Signal.) (The children respond.)
5. (Return to the first word in the column. Present all the words in order until firm.)

EXERCISE 6
Long vowel words

a. (Point to the words in this column.) Read these words the fast way.
b. (Touch the ball for **cape.** Pause two seconds.) Get ready. (Signal.) *Cape.* Yes, **cape.** (Repeat until firm.)
c. (Repeat *b* for **rate** and **note.**)

cape

rate

note

EXERCISE 7
Short vowel words

a. (Point to the words in this column.) Read these words the fast way.
b. (Touch the ball for **cap.** Pause two seconds.) Get ready. (Signal.) *Cap.* Yes, **cap.** (Repeat until firm.)
c. (Repeat *b* for **rat** and **not.**)

cap

rat

not

EXERCISE 8
Short and long vowel words

a. Everybody, read these words again. Remember what you say if there is an **ē** on the end of a word.
b. (Touch the ball for **note.** Pause two seconds.) Get ready. (Signal.) *Note.* Yes, **note.**
c. (Repeat *b* for **cape** and **rat.**)

note

cape

rat

(Repeat any troublesome words.)

Individual test
(Call on individual children. Each child reads a different word.)

Lesson 54

Long-Vowel Words, Short-Vowel Words (Lesson 54)

In lesson 54, a new vowel-rule format is introduced. This format involves a column of long-vowel words, a column of short-vowel words, and a column of short- and long-vowel words.

Corrections

The correction procedure for all words is specified in the box on the format page.

PRACTICE the correction in the box in the format above. Note that step 3 of the correction involves sounding out the misidentified word. When sounding out words that have a final *e*, you do not touch the final e. If the children are to sound out the word *cape*, you touch *c*, *a*, and *p*. In the word *note*, you touch *n*, *o*, and *t*. Practice the correction with these words:

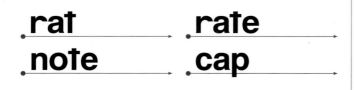

rat   rate

note   cap

- Expect the children to have trouble with exercise 8, in which they read a mix of short- and long-vowel words. You can reduce errors by pausing at least two seconds before saying "Get ready" and signaling.
- If the children make errors on any word, correct, and then return to exercise 6 and present exercises 6, 7, and 8 until the children are perfectly firm.

Track Development

Practice Final-e Rule (Lesson 57)

In lesson 57, two new *Practice final-e rule* formats are introduced. In the first format, shown in exercise 3 on the following page, the children are asked to distinguish when they will say the long vowel sound and when they will not. Then the children read the words the fast way.

Critical Behaviors

To signal for a response in steps *b* and *c*:

1. Point to the ball of the arrow.
2. Ask "Are you going to say the name *ā* when you read this word?"
3. Signal by touching the ball. Do not slash right.

Correction

Follow the correction specified in the format.

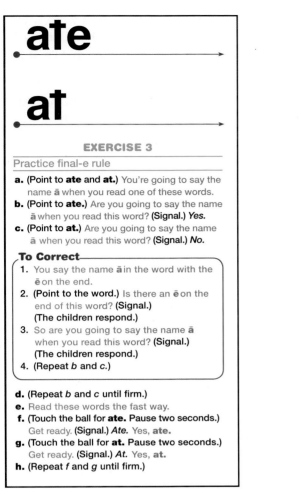

ate

at

EXERCISE 3

Practice final-e rule

a. (Point to **ate** and **at**.) You're going to say the name ā when you read one of these words.

b. (Point to **ate**.) Are you going to say the name ā when you read this word? (Signal.) *Yes.*

c. (Point to **at**.) Are you going to say the name ā when you read this word? (Signal.) *No.*

To Correct

1. You say the name ā in the word with the ē on the end.

2. (Point to the word.) Is there an ē on the end of this word? (Signal.) (The children respond.)

3. So are you going to say the name ā when you read this word? (Signal.) (The children respond.)

4. (Repeat *b* and *c*.)

d. (Repeat *b* and *c* until firm.)

e. Read these words the fast way.

f. (Touch the ball for **ate**. Pause two seconds.) Get ready. (Signal.) *Ate.* Yes, **ate.**

g. (Touch the ball for **at**. Pause two seconds.) Get ready. (Signal.) *At.* Yes, **at.**

h. (Repeat *f* and *g* until firm.)

Lesson 57

The second *Practice final-e rule* format introduced in lesson 57 involves both reading the fast way and sounding out. This format is shown in exercise 9 below.

Note that in step *c*, you touch *h, e,* and *r.* You do not touch the final *e*.

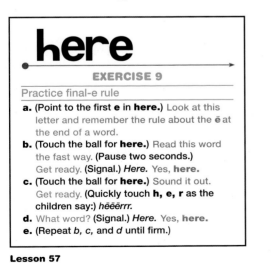

here

EXERCISE 9

Practice final-e rule

a. (Point to the first **e** in **here**.) Look at this letter and remember the rule about the ē at the end of a word.

b. (Touch the ball for **here**.) Read this word the fast way. (Pause two seconds.) Get ready. (Signal.) *Here.* Yes, **here.**

c. (Touch the ball for **here**.) Sound it out. Get ready. (Quickly touch **h, e, r** as the children say:) *hēēērr.*

d. What word? (Signal.) *Here.* Yes, **here.**

e. (Repeat *b, c,* and *d* until firm.)

Lesson 57

Track Development

Two other *Practice final-e rule* formats appear in Block Two. Both of these formats are similar to the format for exercise 9. In the first format, the children do not sound out the word after reading it the fast way. The second format is somewhat abbreviated. In this format, you simply say "Remember to look at the end of the word." You do not mention the *e* on the end of the word.

Read the Fast Way (Lesson 60)

Beginning in lesson 60, words that have a long vowel and a final *e* appear in a *Read the fast way* format.

EXERCISE 11

Read the fast way

a. Read these words the fast way.

b. (Touch the ball for **smiled**. Pause two seconds.) Get ready. (Signal.) *Smiled.* Yes, **smiled.**

c. (Repeat *b* for **more, like, liked, those,** and **here.**)

smiled

more

like

Lesson 60

Corrections

If the children make mistakes in reading words without *d* endings *(more, like),* follow this procedure:

1. Ask: Is there an **e** on the end of the word?

2. Point to the first vowel in the word. What are you going to say for this letter?

3. Touch ball. Sound it out. Get ready. Touch sounds of all letters except the final *e*. Children are to sound the first vowel by sounding the name, not the sound.

(When touching the letters, hold each letter for one second unless it is a stop sound.)

4. Then ask: What word?

PRACTICE the sound-out correction with these words:

rode
made

more
like

Sound Combination (Lesson 45)

In lesson 45, the sound combination *ou* is introduced. The combination is introduced in the formats shown below titled ***ou* as in *out*** and ***ou* word.**

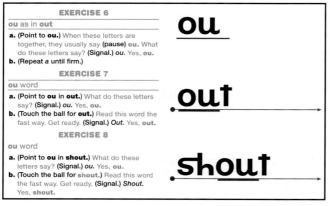

EXERCISE 6

ou as in out

a. (Point to **ou.**) When these letters are together, they usually say (**pause**) **ou.** What do these letters say? (**Signal.**) *ou.* Yes, **ou.**
b. (Repeat *a* until firm.)

EXERCISE 7

ou word

a. (Point to **ou** in **out.**) What do these letters say? (**Signal.**) *ou.* Yes, **ou.**
b. (Touch the ball for **out.**) Read this word the fast way. Get ready. (**Signal.**) *Out.* Yes, **out.**

EXERCISE 8

ou word

a. (Point to **ou** in **shout.**) What do these letters say? (**Signal.**) *ou.* Yes, **ou.**
b. (Touch the ball for **shout.**) Read this word the fast way. Get ready. (**Signal.**) *Shout.* Yes, **shout.**

Lesson 45

Critical Behaviors

Follow the procedures specified on page 23. Remember to pronounce *ou* as "ow."

Disjoining Joined Letters

Beginning in lesson 67, joined letters (such as *th*) become disjoined. Here is a schedule for the letters disjoined in Block Two.

Sound	Lesson
th	67
sh	72
ing	76

All other joined letters will be disjoined in the reading-vocabulary tasks in Block Three.

The format from lesson 67 that introduces the disjoined letters *th* is shown in the next column.

Critical Behaviors

1. In step *a,* show the children the disjoined *th* and tell them that the letters say "ththth" (voiced as in *that;* not unvoiced as in *thing*).

2. In step *c,* point to the familiar words and tell the children that they are going to read them with a disjoined *th.*

3. Steps *d* and *e* are repeated for each word. In *d,* point to the *th* and say "What do these letters say?" Signal by touching under the middle of *th.* Do not slash.

4. In step *e,* touch the ball and say "Read the fast way. Get ready." Signal by slashing right.

th

EXERCISE 11

th words

a. (Point to **th.**) When these letters are together, they usually say **ththth.**
b. What do these letters usually say? (**Signal.**) **ththth.** Yes, **ththth.**
• (Repeat until firm.)
c. (Point to the words.) These are words you already know. See if you can read them when they look this way.
d. (Point to **th** in **the.**) What do these letters say? (**Signal.**) **ththth.**
e. (Touch the ball for **the.**) Read the fast way. Get ready. (**Signal.**) *The.* Yes, **the.**
f. (Repeat *d* and *e* for **them, that,** and **there.**)
g. (Repeat the series of words until firm.)

the

them

that

there

Lesson 67

PRACTICE steps *d* and *e* for each of the words on the page.

Sample: For the word *the,* point just under *th.* Say "What do these letters say?" Signal by touching just under the middle of *th.*

Touch the ball for *the.* "Read the fast way. Get ready." Signal by slashing right.

Corrections—Sounds

- In step *d*, the children may say "the" instead of "ththth."

To correct:

1. Cover *e* and point to *th*. Say: ththth.

2. Ask: What do **these** letters say? Signal by touching under *th*.

3. Uncover *e*. Let's do it again. Point to *th*. What do these letters say?

4. Continue to step *e*.

Corrections—Words

- If children misidentify any word in the list, correct in this way:

1. The word is _____. What word?

2. Point to *th*. What do these letters say?

3. Touch ball for word. Sound it out. Get ready. Move under *th*. Then touch remaining full-sized letters or joined sounds. Children are to identify the *th* as "ththth" when they sound out the word.

4. When sounding out is firm, ask: What word?

5. Return to the word *the* and repeat *e* and *f* in the format for each word.

Samples:

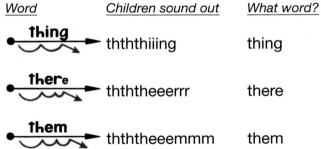

Word	Children sound out	What word?
thing	ththiiing	thing
there	ththeeerrr	there
them	ththeeemmm	them

PRACTICE the sound-out correction with the following words. You will use this correction to correct mistakes on all words in Block Two that become unjoined.

Samples:
Correction for  **shed**

1. The word is **shed.** What word? (Signal.) *Shed.*

2. Point to *sh*. What do these letters say? Touch

under the middle of *sh*. Children respond *shshsh*.

3. Touch ball of arrow. Sound it out. Get ready. Move under *sh, e, d* as children say *shshsheeed*.

4. Return to ball of arrow. What word? Slash right. Children respond *shed.* Yes, **shed.**

Correction for **sing**

1. The word is **sing.** What word? (Signal.) *Sing.*

2. Point to *ing*. What do these letters say? Touch under middle of *ing*. Children respond *iiing*.

3. Touch ball of arrow. Sound it out. Get ready. Move under *s, ing* as children say *sssiiing*.

4. Return to ball of arrow. What word? Slash right. Children respond *sing.* Yes, **sing.**

Practice the sound-out correction with the words above and with the words *when* and *what*. (Remember that *what* is irregular. It is sounded out "whwhwhaaat," but pronounced "whut" or "whot.")

when   **what**

Correcting words with taught sound combination and ed endings:

If the word contains a sound combination that has been taught, use a similar correction.

- **Word to be corrected:** **called**

1. The word is **called.** What word? (Signal.) *Called.*

2. Cover the *ed* endings. Point to *al* in called. What do these letters say? Children respond *all*. Yes, **all.**

3. Touch ball of arrow. Sound it out. Get ready.

4. Move under *c, al.* Children say *call.*

5. Return to ball. What does the first part say? Slash right. Children respond *call.* Yes, **call.**

6. Uncover *ed* ending. Touch ball of arrow. What does it say now? Slash right. Children pronounce word as it is normally pronounced, *calld.* Yes, **called.**

PRACTICE the correction with the words below.
The underscored parts show you what to point to first. (The words you are working with in the teacher presentation materials may not be underscored.)

park**e**d
calle**d**
bark**e**d

wishe**d**
shouted

Note: Ask Step 1 for *sh*.
Repeat step 1 for *ou*.
Then do steps 2 through 5.

Correcting irregular words with ed endings:
If the word is irregular, follow the procedure of having the children sound out and identify the word as it would appear without an ending. Then uncover the ending.

- **Word to be corrected:** **moved**

    For the word *moved,* you would cover only the *d,* have the children sound out "mmmooov-vveee" and identify the first part *(move).* You would then uncover *d.*

    For the word *loved,* follow the same procedure.

- **Word to be corrected:** **touched**

    For the word *touched,* cover the *ed* and have the children sound out and identify *touch.* Then uncover the *ed.*

    Follow this procedure (covering *ed*) for the words *wanted* and *watched.*

Long- and Short-Vowel Words
(Lesson 88)

Beginning in lesson 88, the discrimination of long-vowel and short-vowel words is introduced. Children discriminate between word pairs like *moping* and *mopping.* Earlier in the program, the pronunciation of these words was cued by the Reading Mastery orthography, which has a macron over the vowel if the vowel is long.

Practice the entire format and the correction procedure. Directed application of the correction procedure appears in the program for eight lessons. Use this procedure to correct any mistakes on long- and short-vowel words of this type in word lists for the remainder of the program. To correct the word *timing,* for instance, tell the children: "There's **one m.** The **i** says its name. So the word is **timing.** What word?" Then make sure that you return to the first word in the column and present all the words in order. If you follow this step, the children will learn the discrimination with few errors.

EXERCISE 3A

Rule for words with long and short vowels

a. (Point to **moping** and **mopping.**) Here's a rule for reading these words: If there is only **one p,** the **o** says its name.
b. (Touch the ball for **moping.**) Read this word. (Pause three seconds.) Get ready. (Signal.) *Moping.*
c. (Point to the **p**'s in **mopping.**) This word does not have one **p.** It has **two.** So the **o** does not say its name.
d. (Touch the ball for **mopping.**) Read this word. (Pause three seconds.) Get ready. (Signal.) *Mopping.*
e. (Point to **canned** and **caned.**) Here's a rule for reading these words: If there is only **one n,** the **a** says its name.
f. (Point to the **n**'s in **canned.**) This word does **not** have one **n.** It has **two.** So the **a** does not say its name.
g. (Touch the ball for **canned.**) Read this word. (Pause three seconds.) Get ready. (Signal.) *Canned.*
h. (Point to the **n** in **caned.**) This word has **one n.** (Point to the **a.**) So the **a** says its name.
i. (Touch the ball for **caned.**) Read this word. (Pause three seconds.) Get ready. (Signal.) *Caned.*

To Correct
incorrect vowel sound (**moping**, for example)
1. There is one **p.** The **o** says its name. So the word is **moping.** What word? (Signal.) *Moping.*

OR

There are **two p**'s. The **o** does not say its name. So the word is **mopping.** What word? (Signal.) *Mopping.*
2. (Return to the first word in the column and present all words in order.) Starting over.

moping
mopping
canned
caned
you
tap
tape

j. (Touch the ball for **moping.**) Now you're going to read all of these words the fast way. (Pause two seconds.) Get ready. (Signal.) *Moping.*
k. (Repeat *j* for remaining words in exercise 3A.)

Lesson 88

Two-Part Word (Lesson 44)

In the reading vocabulary, many words appear in the two-part word format. Shown below is an example.

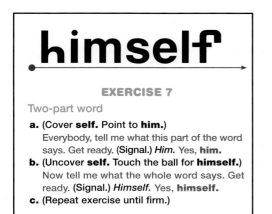

EXERCISE 7
Two-part word

a. (Cover **self**. Point to **him**.)
   Everybody, tell me what this part of the word says. Get ready. (Signal.) *Him.* Yes, **him**.
b. (Uncover **self**. Touch the ball for **himself**.)
   Now tell me what the whole word says. Get ready. (Signal.) *Himself.* Yes, **himself**.
c. (Repeat exercise until firm.)

Lesson 44

Corrections

1. If the children make mistakes on the first part of the word, tell them the whole word. Then have them sound out and identify the first part of the word. Then uncover the remainder of the word.

2. If they miss the second part, tell them the whole word. Then *have them sound out the whole word* and answer the question:
   What word?

PRACTICE this correction with the words below.
The underscored part of the word shows the part that is to be covered.

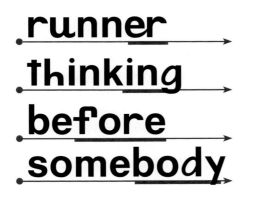

The stories in Block Two average between 170 words around lesson 40 to 273 words by lesson 80.

- As in Block One, the stories incorporate words that have been taught in Reading Vocabulary. Stories 41 through 46 contain many *al-* combination words (*fall, ball, Walter,* and so on).

- Between lessons 47–49 a consolidation occurs with emphasis on hard words, *ar* words, and *al* words reviewed.

- Lessons 50–58 contain many examples of *ou* words (which were previously taught in Reading Vocabulary beginning with lesson 45). One series of 8 stories titled *The Magic Pouch* contains about 129 examples of *ou* words.

- In lesson 59, words that follow the long-vowel rule (and that have no *ed, er,* or *ing* endings) are introduced in the stories with no line over the first vowel and a full-sized *e.* Most of the words that appear between lessons 59 and 75 are not discriminated words (*make, came, fire, lake,* and so on), which means they probably wouldn't be confused with their short-vowel counterpart words.

- Beginning in lesson 76 with a story titled *Sam Gets a Kite Kit,* long-vowel words that must be discriminated from their short-vowel counterparts are introduced. Stories contain such words as *kit* and *kite, tim* and *time, hat* and *hate.* The emphasis remains on this discrimination through Block Two and into Block Three. One series of five stories in Block Three deals with Sid, who has trouble reading long- and short-vowel words. He confuses such words as *can-cane, not-note, pin-pine, pan-pane,* and *slop-slope.* These stories may be difficult for the children, but if the children are firmed on the reading, they will develop the ability to discriminate between words that have a short vowel and those that follow the long-vowel rule.

READ THE ITEMS FOR BLOCK TWO

The only Read the Items in Block Two occurs in lesson 47. The teacher presentation is the same as that presented in Block One. (See page 39.)

WORKSHEETS FOR BLOCK TWO

The following activities appear on the daily Worksheets.
- Story Items
- Reading Comprehension activities
- Following Instructions (Type 1, lessons 40–46); (Type 2, lessons 47–80)
- Sentence Copying—which stops in lesson 48
- Story-Picture Items—a new activity introduced in lesson 61

There are teacher-directed Worksheet activities on only a few lessons. The children work nearly all of the activities independently. A major emphasis of the Worksheet activities in Block Two is placed on the children writing word responses to comprehension items.

Following Instructions Type 1
(Lesson 40)
The first activity that deals with word-writing is following instructions in lesson 40. The format is similar to the following-instructions tasks from Block One, except the children write words, not letters or numbers.

Teacher instructions and the children's activity for the following-instructions exercise in lesson 40 are shown here.

WORKSHEET **40**

FOLLOWING INSTRUCTIONS

The children will need pencils.

EXERCISE 22

Box and circle items

(Children call letters by sounds, not letter names.)
- **a.** (Pass out Worksheet 40 to each child.)
- **b.** (Point to the first circle on side 1.) Everybody, touch this circle. ✔
- **c.** Everybody, touch instruction 1 next to the circle.
- **d.** Reading the fast way. First word. ✔
- • Get ready. (Tap for each word as the children read:) *Make the word sun in the circle.*
- **e.** What does this instruction tell you to do? (Signal.) *Make the word sun in the circle.*

To Correct
Tell the children the answer.
Then repeat *d* and *e*.

- **f.** Everybody, get ready to read instruction 2 next to the circle. First word. ✔
- • Get ready. (Tap for each word as the children read:) *Make the word cat under the circle.*
- **g.** What does this instruction tell you to do? (Signal.) *Make the word cat under the circle.*
- **h.** (Point to the instructions.) Everybody, read the instructions to yourselves. Then do what the instructions tell you to do. ✔
- **i.** You'll follow the instructions for the other circle later.

Lesson 40

1. māke the word sun in the circle.

2. māke the word cat under the circle.

Worksheet 40

If the children are firm on preceding following-instructions tasks, they should have no trouble with this exercise. The teacher instructions appear in only one lesson (40). It is a good idea to watch the children as they work the following instructions in lessons 41 and 42. If the children ask how to work the exercises, do not tell them. Instead, instruct them to read the instructions aloud. Then say, "Do what those instructions tell you to do."

a. (Point to the sentence in the first box on side 2.)

b. Everybody, touch this sentence on your worksheet. ✔

c. I'll read the instructions above the sentence in the box. Listen: **Read this sentence.** That's what you're going to do.

d. Everybody, read the sentence in the box. First word. Get ready. (Tap for each word as the children read:) *The dog was fat.*

e. Everybody, say that sentence without looking. (Signal.) *The dog was fat.*

• (Repeat until firm.)

f. Touch instruction 1 below the sentence in the box. ✔

g. Read that instruction. First word. Get ready. (Tap for each word as the children read:) *Circle the word* **was.**

h. What are you going to do? (Signal.) *Circle the word* **was.**

i. You're going to circle the word **was.** Everybody, the word **was** is in the box. Touch the word **was.** ✔

j. What are you going to do to the word **was**? (Signal.) *Circle it.*

To Correct
1. (Have the children read instruction 1 below the box.)
2. **Then ask,** What are you going to do to the word **was**?

k. Everybody, touch instruction 2 below the sentence in the box. ✔

l. Read that instruction. First word. Get ready. (Tap for each word as the children read:) *Make a line over the word* **the.**

m. What are you going to do? (Signal.) *Make a line over the word* **the.**

n. You're going to make a line over the word **the.** Everybody, touch the word **the** in the box. ✔

o. What are you going to do to the word **the**? (Signal.) *Make a line over it.*

To Correct
1. (Have the children read instruction 2 below the box.)
2. **Then ask,** What are you going to do to the word **the**?

p. Everybody, read instruction 1 to yourself and do what it tells you to do. ✔

q. Everybody, read instruction 2 to yourself and do what it tells you to do. ✔

r. Everybody, you'll follow the instructions for the other sentences later.

Lesson 47

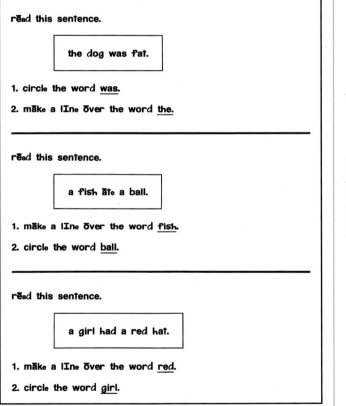

Worksheet 47

In lesson 47, variations of instructions are introduced for two Worksheet activities: Following Instructions and Reading Comprehension.

Following Instructions Type 2
(Lesson 47)

The teacher presentation and the children's material for the new following-instructions activity are shown here.

PRACTICE presenting the format and the corrections that are specified. If the children have mechanical troubles (finding the items under the box, finding the words in the box), repeat the task after correcting the mistakes.

If the children make mistakes on the items for the first following-instructions sentence, structure the presentation on the second sentence. Remember, the structured teacher presentation runs for only one lesson. During this lesson, make the children as firm as possible.

Reading Comprehension
(Lesson 47)

Also in lesson 47, the children begin writing responses to reading-comprehension items. (On preceding tasks in reading-comprehension, the children had merely circled the answers.) The teacher presentation and the children's material for the reading-comprehension story from lesson 47 are shown on the next page.

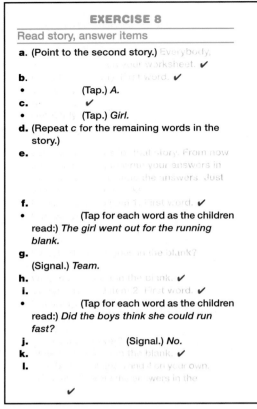

EXERCISE 8

Read story, answer items

a. (Point to the second story.) Everybody,

b.
- (Tap.) *A.*
c. ✔
- (Tap.) *Girl.*
d. (Repeat *c* for the remaining words in the story.)
e.

f.
- (Tap for each word as the children read:) *The girl went out for the running blank.*
g. (Signal.) *Team.*
h. ✔
i. First word. ✔
- (Tap for each word as the children read:) *Did the boys think she could run fast?*
j. (Signal.) *No.*
k. ✔
l.
✔

Lesson 47

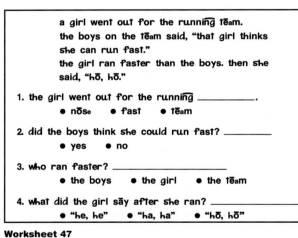

a girl went out for the running team.
the boys on the team said, "that girl thinks
she can run fast."
the girl ran faster than the boys. then she
said, "hŏ, hŏ."

1. the girl went out for the running _____.
   ● nōse   ● fast   ● tēam

2. did the boys think she could run fast? _____
   ● yes   ● no

3. who ran faster? _____
   ● the boys   ● the girl   ● the tēam

4. what did the girl sāy after she ran? _____
   ● "he, he"   ● "ha, ha"   ● "hŏ, hŏ"

Worksheet 47

Note that in the children's material, the blanks are open to provide space for the children to write the answers.

- In steps *b* through *d* of the teacher presentation format, the children read the story about the girl who went out for the running team.
- In step *e,* the teacher tells them that they will write answers in the blanks.
- In step *f,* the children read item 1. *(The girl went out for the running blank.)*
- In step *g,* the children answer the question.

- In step *h,* they write the answer in the blank.
- In steps *i* through *k,* they do item 2 with the teacher.
- In step *l,* they do items 3 and 4 on their own.

Note: There are two reading-comprehension stories in lesson 47, both of which are teacher-directed. This is the only lesson in which the children receive the structured instructions. In following lessons, the children are to work on their own. It is therefore important to make sure that the children are firmed in lesson 47. If they are not, monitor their reading-comprehension work in lessons 48 and 49.

Story Items (Lesson 48)

In lesson 48, the story items are changed so that the children respond by writing answers in the blanks, not by circling answers. (At this point, the reading comprehension and the story items follow the same form. There are blanks in every item. The children write the appropriate answer in the blank.)

The teacher presentation and the story items for lesson 48 are shown below.

Story items
(Point to the story-items exercise.) Today you're going to write the answers in the blanks. Remember, don't circle them. Write them.

Lesson 48

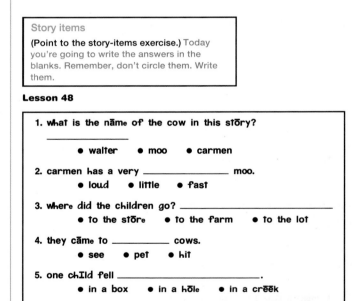

1. what is the nāme of the cow in this stōry?
   _____
   ● walter   ● moo   ● carmen

2. carmen has a very _____ moo.
   ● loud   ● little   ● fast

3. where did the children go? _____
   ● to the stōre   ● to the farm   ● to the lot

4. they cāme to _____ cows.
   ● see   ● pet   ● hit

5. one chĭld fell _____.
   ● in a box   ● in a hōle   ● in a crēēk

Worksheet 48

If possible, monitor the children when they work the story items in lesson 48. If they circle items, show them the blanks and say, "These blanks are open so that you can write in them. That's what you're supposed to do. Find the right answer and write it in the blank."

Spelling Conventions for Reading Comprehension and Story Items

In some of the reading-comprehension activities, the children must compose the answer (not copy it). Follow these rules with regard to their spelling of words:

1. If the word has occurred in the spelling program, the children should be held accountable for spelling it accurately.

2. If the word appears in the choices that are presented with the item, the children should spell the word accurately.

3. The words *yes* and *no* are to be spelled accurately.

4. If the words are in the reading-comprehension story, the children should find the words and spell them accurately.

5. If the item involves writing words that are not on the Worksheet and that have not been presented in the spelling program, do not expect the children to spell all words accurately. Accept phonetic spelling.

Corrections of Spelling Mistakes

If the misspelled word occurs in the reading-comprehension activity, follow this correction:
1. Ask the child to identify the misspelled word.
2. Say: **Find that word in the story.**
3. After the child finds the word, say: **Now write the word the way it is written in the story.**

If the misspelled word is one that occurred earlier in the spelling program, have the child spell the word, following the spelling-program format shown below. Then have the child write the word.

If the children make mistakes in writing the word, use this correction procedure:

1. **(Model)** Here are the sounds in the word **stop.** Listen. **sss** (pause) **t** (pause) **ooo** (pause) **p.**
2. **(Test)** Write the word.

When spelling by letter names begins, use the same correction procedure (model, test), but refer to letter names instead of sounds.

Spelling correction

Award points or some other form of reinforcement for children who make 0 to 2 spelling mistakes on their Worksheet (limited only to words that the children have been taught or should copy).

Following Instructions Type 2
(Lesson 47)

Following Instructions Type 2 begins in lesson 47 and continues through lesson 120. These exercises are different from those in Following Instructions Type 1 (which appeared in Block One). The Type 2 exercises present a sentence in a box. Below the box are items that direct the children to do things to parts of the sentence in the box. The first items instruct the children to circle a specified word: *Circle the word was.* (See page 63.)

Following Instructions Type 2
(Lesson 65)

Beginning in lesson 65, items are introduced in the form, "Circle the word that tells who ate the beans."

Expect some children to have trouble with this type of item. Shown below is the following-directions exercise from lesson 68.

---

sam kissed jill.

1. circle the word that tells who sam kissed.
2. make a line under the word kissed.
3. make a box around the word that tells who kissed jill.

Worksheet 68

Mistake: (item 3)
Some children make a box around the word *jill.*

Corrections

1. Have the children read the sentence in the box aloud.
2. Ask the question: **Who kissed Jill?**
3. Have the children read the item below the box aloud. *(Make a box around the word that tells who kissed jill.)*
4. Say: **Show me the right word in the box.** The children show you the word *sam.* Yes, **Sam.**
5. Read the item to yourself and figure out what you're going to do to the word **Sam.** . . . Do it.

Monitor the children's performance. If you note that they are having trouble with *who* questions, correct the errors. Don't let them accumulate for days.

Following Instructions Type 2
(Lesson 75)

In lesson 75, a new form of item is presented in Following Instructions. For the first time, the children are required to circle more than one word. Expect some children to have trouble.

Jane had a lot of fun at the farm.

1. circle the word that tells who had a lot of fun.

2. circle the words that tell where Jane had fun.

3. make a v̄ over the word had.

Worksheet 75

Mistake: (item 2)
Some children circle *farm.*

Corrections

1. Have the children read the sentence in the box aloud.

2. Ask the question: Where did Jane have fun?

3. Have the children read item 2 aloud. *(Circle the words that tell where jane had fun.)*

4. Say: Show me the right words in the box. The children show you the words *at the farm.*

5. Have the children read the item to themselves and do what the item tells them.

Again, monitor the children's performance and correct errors as soon as they appear.

Story-Picture Items (Lesson 61)

The Story-Picture Items track begins in lesson 61 and continues through Block Two and into Block Three. It sets the stage for a Picture Deductions track in Block Three in which the children are given a rule to apply to a picture. The children apply the rule by circling the appropriate objects in the picture.

The Story-Picture Items track involves questions similar to those presented in the picture-comprehension activities that are introduced every day after the story has been read.

The teacher-presentation format and the story-picture item from lesson 61 are shown below.

Critical Behaviors

1. In step c, the teacher reads the instructions. *(Look at the picture on page 158 of your reader.)* When reading the instructions, read slowly so the children can follow along.

2. In step d, the children read as the teacher taps.

3. In step e, the children tell what they are to do, and they look at the picture.

4. In steps f and g, the children read item 1 *(Does the girl look happy or sad?)*

5. In step h, the children look at the picture and answer the question, "Does the girl look happy or sad?"

6. In step i, the children write the answer in the blank.

★ **STORY-PICTURE ITEMS**
EXERCISE 21

Story picture

a. (Point to the story-picture items exercise on side 2.)

b. Here's something new on your worksheet today. Everybody, touch the instructions. ✔

c. My turn to read the fast way. (Read:) Look at the picture on page 158 of your reader.

d. Your turn to read the instructions the fast way. First word. ✔

• Get ready. **(Tap for each word as the children read:)** *Look at the picture on page 158 of your reader.*

e. Everybody, what do the instructions tell you to do? (Signal.) *Look at the picture on page 158 of my reader.*

• Do it. (Check that the children look at the picture on page 158.)

f. Everybody, touch item 1 below the instructions. ✔

g. Read the fast way. First word. ✔

• Get ready. **(Tap for each word as the children read:)** *Does the girl look happy or sad?*

h. Look at the picture on page 158. Does the girl look happy or sad? (Signal.) *Happy.* Yes, she looks **happy.**

i. Write the answer in the blank. ✔

• (Accept phonetic spelling.)

Lesson 61

---

look at the picture on page 158 of your reader.

1. does the girl look happy or sad? _____

Worksheet 61

Corrections

Expect less proficient children to have trouble understanding the word _or_ in step _h._ If children have trouble with _or,_ follow this correction:

1. Verbally present a series of _or_ questions about the picture. Is the girl sitting or standing? . . . Is the girl sleeping or awake? . . . Is the girl big or little? . . . Is the girl happy or sad?

2. When the children are firm on all questions, have them reread item 1 again. Then ask: Does the girl look happy or sad?

3. After they are firm on answering the question, tell them: Write the answer in the blank.

Block Three

The Textbook Preparation Block
(Lessons 81–160)

In Block Three, the following major activities occur:

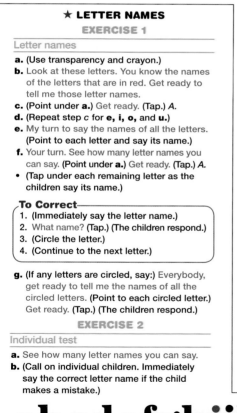

★ **LETTER NAMES**
EXERCISE 1
Letter names

a. (Use transparency and crayon.)
b. Look at these letters. You know the names of the letters that are in red. Get ready to tell me those letter names.
c. (Point under **a.**) Get ready. (Tap.) _A._
d. (Repeat step _c_ for **e, i, o,** and **u.**)
e. My turn to say the names of all the letters. (Point to each letter and say its name.)
f. Your turn. See how many letter names you can say. (Point under **a.**) Get ready. (Tap.) _A._
• (Tap under each remaining letter as the children say its name.)

To Correct
1. (Immediately say the letter name.)
2. What name? (Tap.) (The children respond.)
3. (Circle the letter.)
4. (Continue to the next letter.)

g. (If any letters are circled, say:) Everybody, get ready to tell me the names of all the circled letters. (Point to each circled letter.) Get ready. (Tap.) (The children respond.)

EXERCISE 2
Individual test

a. See how many letter names you can say.
b. (Call on individual children. Immediately say the correct letter name if the child makes a mistake.)

abcdefghijklmnopqrstuvwxyz

Lesson 83

---

1. The children are taught the letter names and the alphabet.

2. The children are taught to identify capital letters.

3. All joined letters become disjoined.

4. The children are taught to identify the sound combination _ea._

5. Traditional textbook print starts in the reading vocabulary at lesson 81. By lesson 92, all stories and Worksheets are written in traditional orthography (no joined letters, small letters, or long lines over the vowels). Capitals appear when appropriate.

6. New tracks occur in the Worksheets:

   Story-Items Review (lessons 101–147)
   Picture Deductions (lessons 95–147)
   Written Deductions Type 1
      (lessons 123–147)
   Written Deductions Type 2
      (lessons 148–160)
   Reading Comprehension of Factual Information
      (lessons 132–160)

LETTER NAMES AND CAPITAL LETTERS

In a series of exercises from lessons 83 to 94, the letter names for the vowels are reviewed, alphabetical order (using lowercase letters) is taught, and the capital letters are introduced.

Letter Names

In Block Three, all lowercase and capital letters are taught by _name,_ not by sound. Letter-names exercises begin in lesson 83 and continue through lesson 86. The track contains three formats. Shown below is the format for letter names and alphabetical order that appears in lesson 83.

Critical Behaviors

The most critical behavior in presenting this format is your timing. The task will be new for some children, but other children will already know the letter names. They will want to rush ahead and say the names quickly.

A good timing when you test the children in step *f* is about one letter name per second.

1. First point to the letter; then touch it.

2. When you touch the letter, the children are to respond.

3. Immediately release your touch.

The children are not to hold the name. For example, they are not to say *efffffff*; they are to say *ef.*

Track Development

In lessons 85 and 86, the letters are not presented in alphabetical order. The children identify each letter.

Capital Letters

Two formats are used to teach the capital letters. One format presents the "easy" capitals; the other presents the "hard" capitals. Easy capital letters are those that closely resemble their lowercase counterparts. Hard capitals *(A, R, D, E, Q, B, L, H, G)* don't resemble their lowercase counterparts.

Introducing Easy Capitals
(Lessons 87–89)

The sixteen "easy" capitals appear in random order in a row on the page. The teacher says, "Capital letters are bigger than the other letters. In a few days, every sentence that you'll read will begin with a capital letter."

Introducing Hard Capitals
(Lessons 89–94)

The "hard" capitals are introduced in two groups. Shown below is the first group *(A, R, D, E, Q),* introduced in lesson 89. The letters appear with their lowercase counterparts for one lesson; then they are reviewed in random order without their lowercase counterparts.

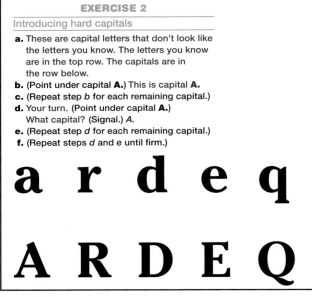

EXERCISE 2

Introducing hard capitals

a. These are capital letters that don't look like the letters you know. The letters you know are in the top row. The capitals are in the row below.
b. (Point under capital **A.**) This is capital **A.**
c. (Repeat step *b* for each remaining capital.)
d. Your turn. (Point under capital **A.**) What capital? (Signal.) *A.*
e. (Repeat step *d* for each remaining capital.)
f. (Repeat steps *d* and *e* until firm.)

a r d e q

A R D E Q

Lesson 89

The same steps are followed for the second group *(B, L, H, G).* In the final format for hard capitals, all the hard capitals are mixed.

Before lesson 94, some capitals *(C, S, V, O, W, P, T, I)* appear in the student materials. *I* is familiar, and the others are similar in upper and lower case except for size and position on the line.

By lesson 94, all sentences and stories in the Storybook and on the Worksheets follow traditional rules for capitalization.

READING VOCABULARY FOR BLOCK THREE

Reading vocabulary is the second activity scheduled for each lesson from lessons 83 to 94 (following letter-names or capital-letters tasks). Reading vocabulary is scheduled as the first activity for lessons 95 to 160.

Reading-Vocabulary Formats

The reading vocabulary for Block Three introduces four word-attack procedures:

1. Reading the fast way without sounding out

2. Reading words that have an underlined part by first reading the underlined part; then reading the whole word the fast way

3. Reading a word the fast way; then spelling the word

4. Spelling a word; then reading it the fast way

Each reading-vocabulary exercise presents four or five columns of words (seven words in a column). All words in a particular column are treated in a particular way. Some columns have words with underlined parts; some have words that are to be read and then spelled. Because each lesson presents between twenty-eight and thirty-five words in reading vocabulary, the teaching of the reading-vocabulary exercises must be fast-paced, with the emphasis on reading, and reading accurately.

Time Frame for Reading Vocabulary

Your goal should be to complete the reading-vocabulary part of the lesson in no more than ten minutes. Within this time, a group that is firm can read the columns of words (from twenty-eight to thirty-five words per lesson) and take individual turns reading a column.

If the children in a group are not firm when they enter Block Three, the reading-vocabulary part of the lesson may take fifteen minutes. Here are some suggestions for improving the reading-vocabulary performance:

1. Enforce the criterion. Be encouraging, but be firm. Praise children for working hard.

2. Use the specified correction procedure, always returning to the first word in the column and repeating the column.

3. If most mistakes are made by the same children, and if those children cannot be moved to a group that is placed at an earlier lesson, give more individual turns, particularly on columns that were very firm during group reading. Don't rush the children; praise accuracy.

4. Present a time challenge to the group. "You're all reading with very few mistakes, just like the big children. Let's see if you can do all the words on these pages in _____ minutes." Time the group. Offer an incentive. For lower-performing groups, first limit your challenge to one column. "This column is hard. Let's see if you can read the whole column without making more than two mistakes." Gradually increase your performance expectation until a group can read all the words in ten minutes or less. Groups that are firm find this part of the lesson very reinforcing, especially when they are timed.

5. Pace your presentation appropriately. Use the information on how fast individuals in the group perform on column reading to adjust the rate at which you present words to the group. Also notice the children's story-reading rate. There should not be great discrepancies between the rate at which they read in the reading-vocabulary exercises and their story-reading rate, although the reading vocabulary will be slightly slower. If there are great discrepancies (reasonable story-reading rate and very slow, drony reading-vocabulary performance), the children don't really understand that you want the same reading behavior on the reading-vocabulary exercises and the story reading. Use challenges to clarify your expectations.

6. Remember to wait until the end of the reading-vocabulary part of the lesson to give individual turns.

Note: If your group is large, not all children will get a turn to read a column each day. In this situation, be sure that you do call on the lower-performing children more frequently than higher performers.

Transition (Lessons 81–83)

During lessons 81 to 83, stories and Worksheet exercises are still written in Reading Mastery orthography. Reading-vocabulary words, however, are presented in traditional print. The teacher introduces the new print by telling the children, "The words on this page have letters that look a little different. Also, there are no lines over any letters." The children then read the words.

Note: Traditional print appears in the Storybook at lesson 84 and in the Workbook at lesson 86.

Correction Procedure

(Lessons 81–90)

After lesson 91 you will use a spelling correction for all reading-vocabulary errors. However, during lessons 81 to 90 (before the children are firm on letter names), use the correction procedure shown below. In following this procedure, you identify the correct word; the children identify the word; then you return to the first word in the column and present all words in order.

- The correct word is *cone.* The children say *con.*

> **To Correct**
> word-identification errors
> (**cone,** for example)
> 1. That word is **cone.** What word? (Signal.) *Cone.*
> 2. (Return to the first word in the column and present all words in order.) *Starting over.*

Lesson 81

Note: If the mistake occurs on an individual turn, always present the correction to the group. Then direct the individual to start over and read all the words in the column.

PRACTICE the above correction. Remember to correct all reading-vocabulary errors in lessons 81 to 90 with this correction. Do not use the sounding out or long-vowel rule corrections. In Block Three you are working on firming up the children's ability to read all words the fast way.

Spelling by Letter Names

All letter names are taught by lesson 86. Starting with lesson 86, the children apply their spelling skills to words they read. Spelling improves word identification because spelling forces attention to every letter in a word.

READING VOCABULARY

EXERCISE 3

Spelling by letter names

a. My turn to spell some of these words by saying the letter names.

b. (Touch the ball for **gave.**) My turn. (Tap under each letter as you say:) **G-A-V-E.**

c. (Touch the ball for **here.**) My turn. (Tap under each letter as you say:) **H-E-R-E.**

d. (Touch the ball for **when.**) My turn. (Tap under each letter as you say:) **W-H-E-N.**

e. Your turn to spell all the words in this column by letter names.

f. (Touch the ball for **gave.**) Spell by letter names. Get ready. (Tap under each letter as children say:) *G-A-V-E.*

g. (Repeat step *f* for each remaining word in the column.)

h. (Repeat any words on which children make mistakes.)

i. Now you're going to read all the words in this column the fast way.

j. (Touch the ball for **gave.**) Get ready. (Slash.) *Gave.*

k. (Repeat step *j* for each remaining word in the column.)

l. (Repeat steps *j* and *k* until firm.)

gave

here

when

bug

because

doing

came

Lesson 86

Signals

In all spelling formats, the teacher signals by tapping under each letter in the word.

- Steps *a* through *d* of the introductory format shown above model the spelling of some of the words.
- In steps *e* through *h,* the children spell all the words in the column.
- Steps *i* through *l* direct the children to read all the words in the column the fast way. After completing the column, the children will either reread the column (until firm) or go to the next column.

Corrections

If the children say the incorrect letter name in steps *f* through *h,* tell them the name and repeat the step.

Track Development

Several formats in reading vocabulary involve spelling. Four of them are described below.

Children Spell, Then Read
(Lessons 88–160)

The words in this format are familiar and have usually been presented several times in other formats. Children spell each word and then read it.

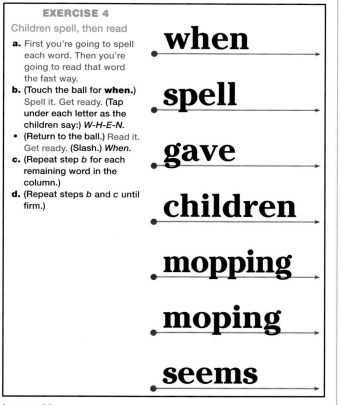

EXERCISE 4
Children spell, then read

a. First you're going to spell each word. Then you're going to read that word the fast way.
b. (Touch the ball for **when**.) Spell it. Get ready. (Tap under each letter as the children say:) *W-H-E-N.*
• (Return to the ball.) Read it. Get ready. (Slash.) *When.*
c. (Repeat step *b* for each remaining word in the column.)
d. (Repeat steps *b* and *c* until firm.)

when
spell
gave
children
mopping
moping
seems

Lesson 95

Words Beginning with Capital Letters (lessons 91–94)

Each word in the column begins with a capital letter. Children do not say "capital" when they spell words with capital letters. For example, they spell the word Ann, *a-n-n* (not *"capital" a-n-n*). After lesson 94, words with capitals are mixed in with words that begin with lowercase letters.

Read the Fast Way (Lessons 81–160)

Children have been reading a variation of this format since the beginning of the program. The only change is the correction procedure. Beginning with lesson 91, you will use the spelling correction shown after exercise 1 in the right-hand column of this page.

Teacher Reads the Words in Red
(Lessons 81–160)

Some words in the column are red; some are black. The red words are usually new or difficult words. The teacher first identifies the red words; then the children spell them (steps *a* through *d* of the format from lesson 95 shown below). In the last part of the format (steps *e* through *h*), the children return to the first word in the column and read all the words.

READING VOCABULARY
EXERCISE 1
Teacher reads the words in red

a. I'll read each word in red. Then you'll spell each word.
b. (Touch the ball for **Ann**.) My turn. (Slash as you say:) Ann. What word? (Signal.) *Ann.*
c. (Return to the ball.) Spell it. Get ready. (Tap under each letter as the children say:) *A-N-N.*
• What word did you spell? (Signal.) *Ann.*
d. (Repeat steps *b* and *c* for each word in red.)
e. Your turn to read all the words in this column.
f. (Touch the ball for **Ann**. Pause.) Get ready. (Slash.) *Ann.*
g. (Repeat step *f* for each remaining word in the column.)
h. (Repeat steps *f* and *g* until firm.)

Ann
Dan
lucky
early
They
One
from

Lesson 95

PRACTICE exercise 1 with another adult. At step *g,* your partner misidentifies the word *one.* Since this is lesson 95 and your spelling correction starts at 91, use the spelling correction shown for *note* on page 72, To correct, steps 1–5.

Note: If the mistake occurs on an individual turn, always present the correction to the group. Then direct the individual to start over and read all the words in the column.

Words with Underlined Parts
(Lesson 81–160)

At least one column of words in every lesson presents words with underlined parts. Children read the underlined part; then they read the whole word. This procedure is used for many types of words: compound words (may<u>be</u>, <u>him</u>self, some<u>body</u>, or <u>some</u>body); words with sound combinations (<u>th</u>em, <u>le</u>ave, <u>sh</u>out, or sh<u>out</u>); words that follow the long-vowel rule with endings (<u>hope</u>d, <u>hopp</u>ed, <u>tape</u>d); and words with various endings (<u>dimes</u>, <u>start</u>ing, <u>we</u>'ll, <u>closer</u>, <u>dress</u>ed, <u>poor</u>est).

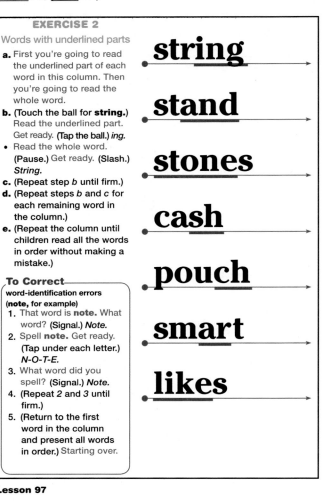

EXERCISE 2
Words with underlined parts

a. First you're going to read the underlined part of each word in this column. Then you're going to read the whole word.

b. (Touch the ball for **string.**) Read the underlined part. Get ready. (Tap the ball.) *ing.*
• Read the whole word. (Pause.) Get ready. (Slash.) *String.*

c. (Repeat step *b* until firm.)

d. (Repeat steps *b* and *c* for each remaining word in the column.)

e. (Repeat the column until children read all the words in order without making a mistake.)

To Correct
word-identification errors
(**note**, for example)
1. That word is **note.** What word? (Signal.) *Note.*
2. Spell **note.** Get ready. (Tap under each letter.) *N-O-T-E.*
3. What word did you spell? (Signal.) *Note.*
4. (Repeat *2* and *3* until firm.)
5. (Return to the first word in the column and present all words in order.) *Starting over.*

str<u>ing</u>

st<u>and</u>

<u>st</u>ones

ca<u>sh</u>

pou<u>ch</u>

<u>sm</u>art

<u>like</u>s

Lesson 97

• In step *a* of the format, you introduce the column and tell the children what they will do: "First you're going to read the underlined part of each word in this column. Then you're going to read the whole word."

• In step *b* you'll use two signals. To signal a response to the underlined part, <u>tap the ball.</u> Tapping the ball requires the children to analyze the underlined part in the context of the whole word. To signal a response to the whole word, <u>slash right</u> (as you do for any fast-way reading).

PRACTICE exercise 2 above. Your partner will not make mistakes. Be sure that you pause between the instructions "Read the whole word" and "Get ready" to provide time for the reader to think.

Corrections

Expect mistakes in this format, especially with words that follow the long-vowel rule. The children make two major mistakes in step *b*—misidentifying the underlined part and misreading the whole word.

Correction for misreading the underlined part:

Sample. For the underlined part of the word ca<u>sh</u>, the children say *ch.*

1. The underlined part is **shshsh.** What's the underlined part? Tap the ball. *Shshsh.*

2. Spell **shshsh.** Get ready. Tap the ball for each letter. *s-h.*

3. What does the underlined part say? Tap the ball. *Shshsh.*

4. Repeat 2 and 3 until firm.

5. Present step *b* for the word cash.

6. Return to the first word in the column and present all words in order. Starting over.

PRACTICE the correction for the underlined part of the word ca<u>sh</u>. Practice the same correction for the word <u>st</u>ones. Your partner is to say *store* for the underlined part.

Correction for misreading the whole word:

Sample. For the word <u>hope</u>d, the children say *hopped.*

1. That word is **hoped.** What word? (Signal.) *Hoped.*

2. Spell **hoped.** Get ready. Tap under each letter. *H-o-p-e-d.*

3. What word did you spell? (Signal.) *Hoped.*

4. Repeat 2 and 3 until firm.

5. Return to the first word in the column and present all words in order. Starting over.

PRACTICE the correction for the word <u>hoped</u>.
Your partner is to say *hopped*.

Note: During lessons 81 to 94, children are reading stories in which long-vowel words and short-vowel words are paired. Word pairs, like *tap* and *tape, mop* and *mope, mopped* and *moped,* are read in the stories. Children usually have less difficulty reading those words in the stories than they do in the reading vocabulary. Expect only occasional errors on words that follow the long-vowel rule after lesson 95.

PRACTICE the reading-vocabulary part of Lesson 105 on pages 97 and 98 until you feel confident. Anticipate mistakes. Test yourself. See if you can run all the exercises, with and without mistakes, in five minutes. Remember to confirm all words that are read correctly by the group (as you have been doing in Blocks One and Two). For example, immediately after the word string is read, say, "Yes, string."

STORY READING FOR BLOCK THREE

- Block Three contains many serial stories. The longest are the Ott and Carla stories and the Jean stories. Each series runs for fifteen lessons.
- The stories in the block average about 315 words.
- Some of the stories involve plays on words, especially the Ott and Carla stories in lessons 112 to 126 and the Kim stories in lessons 127 to 130. Often, the lower-performing children are able to read the stories but fail to catch the significance of things that happen. For example, Kim tries to call for a *van* to move her stuff. However, she looks up *vane* in the phone book and gets a weather vane instead of a van. When such situations occur, <u>model</u> <u>the reaction you want from the children.</u> "Oh, that silly Kim. She didn't want a vane, did she? I sure wish she could read better."

  Follow this procedure whenever the children fail to react to something that they would probably find amusing. <u>You</u> react. When you reread the story, you will find that the children will react in the way you did.
- The vocabulary of the stories continues to follow the reading vocabulary in the lessons.
- Individual Fluency Checkouts continue. At lesson 160, the last lesson in the program, children who pass the Fluency Checkout read at least ninety words per minute.

Story Format (Lessons 81–83)

Stories 81, 82, and 83 are the last stories presented in *Reading Mastery* orthography. At lesson 81, there is a major change in the procedures you use to direct the children's story reading.

EXERCISE 10

First reading

a. Everybody, get ready to read the story. Touch the title of the story. ✔
- We're going to read this story two times. The second time, I'll ask questions.

b. I'm going to call on individual children to read two or three sentences. Everybody, follow along. If you hear a mistake, raise your hand. Children who do not have their place lose their turn. **(Call on individual children to read two or three sentences. Do not ask comprehension questions.)**

To Correct
word-identification errors **(from, for example)**
1. That word is **from.** What word? *From.*
2. Go back to the beginning of the sentence and read the sentence again.

EXERCISE 11

Second reading

a. Everybody, you're going to read the story again. This time, I'm going to ask questions. Touch the title of the story. ✔
b. (Call on individual children to read two or three sentences. Ask the specified questions at the end of each underlined sentence.)

Lesson 81

Individual reading replaces group reading. Group reading of the story is dropped. Children have been reading individually for their checkout on Fluency: Rate/Accuracy every five lessons since lesson 5. Individual children now read two or three sentences for each reading turn. Children who lose their place lose their turn.

Story Format (Lessons 84–160)

The children begin Storybook 2 at lesson 84. The stories are now presented in traditional textbook print. Also at lesson 84, there is a major change in the story-reading presentation procedures. The presentation format from lesson 85 is shown on page 74.

Five-Error Mark

Note the big red circled 5 in the story. The red 5 denotes the five-error mark. You will tally each error as individual children read.

If the group makes no more than five errors by the time it reaches the five-error mark, you will reread the story to the children from the beginning to the five-error mark, stopping at the end of each underlined sentence to ask the specified comprehension questions.

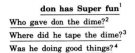

don has Super fun[1]

Who gave don the dime?[2]

Where did he tape the dime?[3]

Was he doing good things?[4]

EXERCISE 11

Reading—decoding

a. Everybody, look at the story on page 4.

b. Everybody, in the middle of the story there's a big red number 5 in a circle. Touch that number 5. ✔

• That 5 tells you that, if the group reads all the way to the 5 without making more than five errors, we can go on in the story. But if the group makes more than five errors, you have to go back and read the first part again. You have to keep reading it until you can read it without making more than five errors. I'll count the errors. I'll tell you about the big star later.

c. Everybody, touch the title of the story. ✔

d. I'm going to call on individual children to read two or three sentences. Everybody, follow along. If you hear a mistake, raise your hand. Children who do not have their place lose their turn. (Call on individual children to read two or three sentences. Do not ask comprehension questions.)

To Correct

word-identification errors (from, for example)

1. That word is **from**. What word? *From.*
2. Go back to the beginning of the sentence and read the sentence again.
3. (Tally all errors.)

e. (If the children make more than five errors: when they reach the 5, say:) You made too many errors. Go back to the beginning of the story and we'll try again. Try to read more carefully this time. (Call on individual children to read two or three sentences. Do not ask comprehension questions. Repeat step e until firm, and then go on to step f.)

Lesson 85

---

did don mope after he became a super man?[5]

don was hopping around the store in his cap and his cape. he was hitting the walls and making holes. he was having a lot of fun.

all at once he stopped. he said, "I will go outside and show what a super man I am."[6]

When don left the store, he didn't open the door. he ran into the door. "Crash."[7]

Some boys were standing outside the store. They said, "look at that funny man in a cap and a cape."

★ don said, "I am no funny man. I am a super man."

---

f. (When the children read to the number 5 without making more than five errors: say:) Good reading. I'll read the story from the beginning to the 5 and ask you some questions. (Read the story, starting with the title. Stop at the end of each underlined sentence and ask the specified question. When you reach the 5, call on individual children to continue reading the story. Have each child read two or three sentences. Ask the specified questions at the end of each underlined sentence.)

[1] What's Don going to do in this story? (Signal.) *Have super fun.*

[2] Everybody, say that question. (Signal.) *Who gave Don the dime?*

• What's the answer? (Signal.) *The woman.*

[3] What's the answer? (Signal.) *To his arm.*

[4] Say that question. (Signal.) *Was he doing good things?*

---

don ran to a car that was parked near the store.[8] he picked the car up and gave it a big heave.[9] The car crashed into another car. ⑤

The boys yelled, "let's get out of here. That man is a nut."

"Come back," don shouted. "let me show you how super I am."

but the boys did not come back. They ran as fast as they could go.[10]

don said, "I think I will fly to the top of this store." So he did.[11] Then he said, "I think I will dive down to the street." So he did. he took a dive. "Crash." he made a big hole in the street.[12]

"This is a lot of fun," don said.[13]

To be continued[14]

• What's the answer? (Signal.) *No.*

[5] What's the answer? (Signal.) *No.*

[6] What's he going to do? (Signal.) *Go outside and show what a super man he is.*

[7] What went crash? (Signal.) *The door.*

• Why? (The children respond.)

[8] What do you think he'll do to that car? (The children respond.)

• Let's find out.

[9] What did he do to the car? (The children respond.)

[10] Who ran? (Signal.) *The boys.*

• Why did they run? (The children respond.)

• I don't blame them. I'd run away, too.

[11] What did he do? (Signal.) *Fly to the top of the store.*

[12] How did the hole get in the street? (The children respond.)

[13] What did he say? (Signal.) *This is a lot of fun.*

[14] Will there be more Don stories? (Signal.) *Yes.*

The children then take turns reading from the five-error mark to the end of the story. Do not tally errors for this part, but continue to ask the comprehension questions. Note that the children read the complete story only one time and you read to the 5 one time.

PRACTICE presenting the format to your partner, who makes errors. When you reach step e, decide whether you should reread the story from the beginning to the 5 and ask the specified comprehension questions or if you should direct your partner back to the beginning of the story.

The format for directing story reading becomes less detailed at lesson 87, but the procedures are the same.

How to Read the Story to the Children

Children are very reinforced by this activity. The children should follow along with their finger or a marker as you read. Encourage the children to look up when you ask a question but to "keep their place" with their finger or marker.

One of your major goals in reading the story to the children is to model inflection, appropriate responses to story content and rate. Adjust your rate so that you read to them a little faster—but only a little faster—than you expect them to read on their individual Fluency Checkouts. (That time is specified in the Fluency Checkouts.) A good way to know if you're reading at an appropriate rate is to watch the

---

children's fingers as they follow along. If their fingers are not in place, you're probably reading too fast. Never read to them as fast as you would if you were reading a story aloud during library time.

PRACTICE timing yourself on story 85. Start with the title and read to the five-error mark. There are 147 words. You should read this section (without asking questions for this practice) in a little over two minutes.

Fluency Checkouts: Rate/Accuracy (Lessons 85–160)

In Blocks One and Two, you specified the part of the story the children were to read for their individual Fluency Checkouts. Starting at story 85, every Fluency Checkout story is marked with a star (in addition to the five-error mark). The children read to the star for their individual Fluency Checkouts.

The "Rule" Stories (Lessons 146–160)

The culmination of work in *Reading Mastery*, Grade 1 is the series of stories that runs from lesson 146 through 160. These stories contain all the types of words that have been taught. The stories also involve all the comprehension skills that have been taught. The stories are about Jean, who dreams that she is in a strange land—the "Land of Peevish Pets". Before she can leave the land, she must learn sixteen rules that hold for this strange land. The rules are presented in the stories.

Shown is a passage from story 146 and the comprehension questions that pertain to the passage.

Critical Behaviors

The rules presented in each story are used in subsequent stories. Therefore, it is important to firm them when they appear in the story.

The rule in story 146 is, "All little crumps are mean." Follow these procedures for firming this rule:

1. *Lead:* "Everybody, say that rule with me." Set a cadence or rhythm for presenting rules. The children will learn to say them faster with a cadence as a prompt. A good idea is to divide the rule into two parts. For example, "All <u>little</u> crumps (pause pause) are mean."

2. *Test:* "All by yourselves. Get ready." Signal.

---

that seemed to be singing. <u>And right in the middle of her dream was an old wizard.</u>[5]

"Ho, ho," the wizard said to her. "What is your name?"

"Jean," she answered.

"Well, Jean," he said, "I hope you have a fine time here in the land of peevish pets."

"What are little crumps?" Jean asked.

"That doesn't matter," the wizard answered. "Just remember the rule: <u>All little crumps are mean.</u>"[7]

Jean said, "I'll remember that rule: <u>All crumps are mean.</u>"[8]

"No, no," the wizard said. "All <u>little</u> crumps are mean."

"I've got it," Jean said. "But what and when . . . ."

<u>The wizard was gone, and Jean was all alone in the land of peevish pets.</u>[9]

More to come

---

[5] Who did she meet in her dream? **(Signal.)** *An old wizard.* Yes, a wizard does magic.

[6] Everybody, say that rule with me. **(Signal. Teacher and children say:)** *All little crumps are mean.*

• (Repeat until firm.) All by yourselves. Get ready. **(Signal. The children repeat the rule until firm.)**

[7] Everybody, what's the rule? **(Signal.)** *All little crumps are mean.*

[8] What did Jean say about crumps? **(Signal.)** *All crumps are mean.*

• Is that right? **(Signal.)** *No.* What's the rule? **(Signal.)** *All little crumps are mean.* Right. All little crumps are mean.

[9] What happened to the wizard? **(The children respond.)**

• Was Jean alone? **(Signal.)** *Yes.*

• Next time we'll read more about the crumps.

Lesson 146

Expect lower-performing children to require perhaps ten repetitions on rules before they are firm in saying them. <u>Give them the repetition the first time the rule appears.</u>

PRACTICE presenting the rule as you lead in step 1. Use the cadence specified.

"Rules" from Stories 146–160

Here are suggested cadence and emphases for presenting other rules in the peevish pets sequence.

- If you say, "Away, away," (pause pause) a <u>mean</u> crump will go away.
- Every <u>dusty</u> path (pause pause) leads to the <u>lake</u>.
- Every <u>rocky</u> path (pause pause) leads to the <u>mountain</u>.
- Red food is good to eat.
- If you eat <u>three</u> red bananas, (pause pause) you get red <u>stripes</u>.
- If you jump in the lake, (pause pause) the stripes will <u>disappear</u>.
- If you stand on <u>one foot</u>, (pause pause) the <u>white hair</u> will disappear.
- If you want your hair back, (pause pause) clap your hands.
- If you want to be warm again, (pause pause) you say, (pause) "I want to be warm again."
- If you want to be cold, (pause pause) say, "Side, slide."
- Talking animals lie.
- If you tap your foot three times, (pause pause) you will fly.
- If you tell him to become a dog, (pause pause) he becomes the letters d-o-g.
- If you want the wizard to disappear, (pause pause) you say, "But what and when."
- If you want the wizard to appear, (pause pause) call for help.

Rule Review (Lessons 147–160)

The rule-review exercise is presented before each story. In lesson 147, the rule, "All little crumps are mean," is reviewed. Each of the sixteen rules is reviewed several times. If you firm the children when a rule is first presented, they should have few problems with rule applications.

Shown below is the rule-review format for lesson 151. It reviews three rules.

RULE REVIEW
EXERCISE 5

Rule review

a. Everybody, you have learned rules in the earlier Jean stories.

b. You learned a rule about every dusty path. Say that rule. Get ready. **(Signal.)** *Every dusty path leads to the lake.*

- **(Repeat until firm.)**

c. You learned a rule about every rocky path. Say that rule. Get ready. **(Signal.)** *Every rocky path leads to the mountain.*

- **(Repeat until firm.)**

d. You learned a rule about red food. Say that rule. Get ready. **(Signal.)** *Red food is good to eat.*

- **(Repeat until firm.)**

e. (If the children missed any rules, repeat steps *b* through *d*.)

Lesson 151

Although the rules in the "Land of Peevish Pets" are silly and may seem to have little bearing on reading skills, they present a reinforcing task to the children quite similar to the ones they will later encounter in textbooks.

1. The children learn a system of information, not merely a single fact or isolated bits of information.

2. They apply the information from story to story and from situation to situation. What is learned now, in other words, is applied later to other situations in the system.

3. The only difference between the rules in this series of stories and the rules that children learn in science and social studies is that the rules from the "Land of Peevish Pets" are embedded in a story. Although names such as "crumps" are nonsense words, the process of learning the meaning of these words is no different from that involved with any unfamiliar word.

READ THE ITEMS FOR BLOCK THREE

Read-the-items exercises appear in lessons 81 through 94 in Block Three. The teacher presentation is the same as that presented in Block One. (See page 39.) The items become more difficult in Block Three. Below are some of the items from this block:

> *Say "spot" if the teacher says "stop."*
> *When the teacher says "saw," say "was."*
> *If the teacher says "pin," say "pine."*

These items are designed to contain words that are easily confused. To reduce errors on these items:

1. Warn the children that the item is difficult. "You'll have to read the item carefully today. It's hard."

2. If the children made mistakes on other items, have them reread the difficult items before playing the game.

3. Say the item immediately before the game. (See the instructions on page 42, *Correction for Reading Mistakes.*)

4. When playing the game, give the children thinking time before presenting the signal.

If the children make mistakes, use the correction procedures outlined in the format and amplified on page 42, *Corrections for Exercise 3 (Playing the Game).*

WORKSHEETS FOR BLOCK THREE

During Block Three, a new track—Deductions—is introduced (lessons 95–160). Throughout the block there are story-items and reading-comprehension activities; however, changes occur in both of these tracks. In the story-items track, story-items review questions are introduced beginning in lesson 101 and continuing through lesson 147. The review items refer to stories that were read earlier in the block. The goal of the review exercises is to prompt the children to become facile in remembering information from day to day. In reading comprehension, nonfiction factual passages are introduced in lesson 132. These passages give the children practice in reading material that is designed to teach them something new. This skill is particularly important in reading textbooks.

Following-instructions exercises appear in the block through lesson 120, at which time they stop. On the following day, some of the procedures that had been used in following instructions become incorporated in the story-items exercises.

Following Instructions Type 2
(Lesson 85)

Children may encounter problems in the Following Instructions Type 2 track at lesson 85. In this lesson, *how* questions are introduced:

Worksheet 85

Corrections

The children often have trouble because they can't find the word *how* in the sentence. After they read the sentence, ask: Jill felt **how?** The children respond: *Sad.* Yes, **how** did Jill feel? Then follow the steps specified in the correction for *who* or *where* questions.

Deductions

The Deductions track begins in lesson 95 and continues through lesson 160. Three types of deduction exercises are included in the track—one picture deduction and two types of written deductions.

Picture Deductions
(Lessons 95–147)

Picture deductions are introduced first. The format that introduces the exercise in lesson 95 and the related Worksheet activity are shown below.

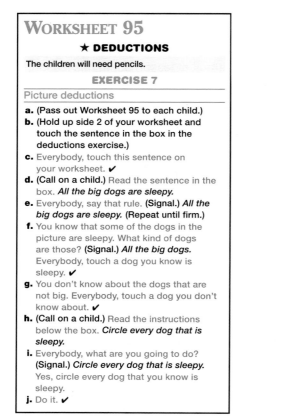

WORKSHEET 95

★ DEDUCTIONS

The children will need pencils.

EXERCISE 7

Picture deductions

a. (Pass out Worksheet 95 to each child.)

b. (Hold up side 2 of your worksheet and touch the sentence in the box in the deductions exercise.)

c. Everybody, touch this sentence on your worksheet. ✔

d. (Call on a child.) Read the sentence in the box. *All the big dogs are sleepy.*

e. Everybody, say that rule. (Signal.) *All the big dogs are sleepy.* (Repeat until firm.)

f. You know that some of the dogs in the picture are sleepy. What kind of dogs are those? (Signal.) *All the big dogs.* Everybody, touch a dog you know is sleepy. ✔

g. You don't know about the dogs that are not big. Everybody, touch a dog you don't know about. ✔

h. (Call on a child.) Read the instructions below the box. *Circle every dog that is sleepy.*

i. Everybody, what are you going to do? (Signal.) *Circle every dog that is sleepy.* Yes, circle every dog that you know is sleepy.

j. Do it. ✔

Lesson 95

All the big dogs are sleepy.

Circle every dog that is sleepy.

Worksheet 95

Critical Behaviors

- In step *e,* the children are firmed on reading and saying the rule: *All the big dogs are sleepy.* Children who are less proficient in language skills may require quite a few repetitions.

Corrections for Steps *f* and *g*

In steps *f* and *g* correct any mistakes this way:

1. What's the rule? The children respond *All the big dogs are sleepy.* Yes, **all the big dogs are sleepy.**

2. Point to the dog. Everybody, is this dog big? . . . So do you know if this dog is sleepy?

Note: Children may respond to little dogs in the following way:

Teacher: Is this dog big?
Children: *No.*
Teacher: So is this dog sleepy?
Children: *I don't know.* (Accept this response.)
Teacher: Good thinking. The rule only tells about the big dogs.

Track Development

The teacher-directed presentation on picture-deduction items runs from lesson 95 through lesson 99. After lesson 99, the children work independently. The rules that are presented through lesson 131 are in one of the following forms:

All _____ are _____.
(This is the form of the rule in Worksheet 95 shown here—*All the big dogs are sleepy.*)

Every _____ is _____.
(*Every white box is made of wood.*)

If _____ then _____.
(*If a horse is running, it is old.*)
(*If a cup has spots, it is hot.*)

If children have trouble on the teacher-directed presentations, monitor their performance when they work independently. The children may make a variety of mistakes.

Corrections for Picture Deductions
(Lessons 95–131)

1. If the children circle the wrong pictures, have them read the rule aloud, say the rule without reading it, and answer questions about each picture.

2. If they don't follow the instructions (making boxes around the horses when the instructions direct them to circle the horses), have them read the instructions aloud and then do what the instructions tell them to do.

Picture Deductions
(Lessons 132–147)

Beginning at lesson 132, rules with two criteria are introduced. For example:

Every man with a hat will go fishing.
Jane will buy every bottle that is little and round.
Every dog with long ears is named Sandy.

Corrections for Picture Deductions
(Lesson 132–147)

If children have trouble with the two-criteria rules, use a firming procedure similar to that specified in steps *f* and *g* on the format for lesson 95.

For example, if the children have trouble with the item, *Every man with a hat will go fishing:*

1. Have the children read the rule aloud and then say it without reading it.

2. Point to each man and ask: **Is this a man with a hat?** Stress *with a hat.*

3. Then ask: So will this man go fishing?

If the children are unable to answer the first question, break the question into two parts:

1. Is this a man? . . . Does he have a hat?

2. Then ask: So will this man go fishing?

Written Deductions

In lesson 123, written deductions are introduced. They continue through the end of the block. Written deductions are similar to picture deductions except that they require the children to work from a written description of the examples, not from pictures.

Written Deductions Type 1
(Lessons 123–160)

The Written Deductions Type 1 track begins in lesson 123 and continues through lesson 160. Shown below are the teacher presentation and the Worksheet activity for the written-deductions item from lesson 124.

> ### EXERCISE 8
> Written deductions
>
> **a.** (Pass out Worksheet 124 to each child.)
> **b.** (Hold up side 2 of your worksheet and touch the sentence, "Every dog pants," in the deductions exercise.)
> **c.** Everybody, touch this sentence on your worksheet. ✔
> **d.** I'm going to call on different children to read a sentence. Everybody, follow along.
>   1. (Call on a child.) Read the sentence in the box. *Every dog pants.*
>   • Everybody, what do you know about every dog? (Signal.) *It pants.* Yes, it pants.
>   2. (Call on a child.) Read the sentence next to the box. *Rob is a dog.*
>   • Everybody, what do you know about Rob? (Signal.) *He is a dog.*
>   • And what do you know about every dog? (Signal.) *It pants.*
>   3. (Call on a child.) Read the sentence under the box. **What does Rob do?**
>   • Everybody, listen. Every dog pants. Rob is a dog. So, what does he do? (Signal.) *He pants.* Yes, he pants.
> **e.** Let's do that problem again. (Repeat the sentence reading and questions in step *d.*)
> **f.** Everybody, write the answer in the blank. ✔

Lesson 124

Every dog pants.	Rob is a dog.
What does Rob do? _____	

Worksheet 124

Be sure that you practice this format until you can present it without looking at the page.

Critical Behaviors

1. When you present the format to the children, make sure that you firm them on step *d.* For some of the children, this may be the first time they have heard a conclusion of this type. Make sure they hear it frequently enough to become familiar with it.

PRACTICE steps *b* through *f* in the format from lesson 124. Also practice it with these rules from lessons 127 and 129:

All children go to school.	Tom and Linda are children.
What do Tom and Linda do? _____	

Every glip is red.	Tom is a glip.
What do you know about Tom? _____	

Corrections for Written Deductions Type 1

If the children make mistakes, ask them a "What do you know about . . .?" question for each sentence in the task. For example:

Every glip is red.
Tom is a glip.
What do you know about Tom?

1. Ask: What do you know about every glip? The children respond: *It's red.*

2. Ask: What do you know about Tom? The children respond: *He's a glip.*

3. Ask: So what else do you know about Tom? The children respond: *He's red.*

PRACTICE the above correction. Then practice the correction with these rules:

Every car has doors.
Sid has a car.
What does Sid's car have?

The rules presented in this track are very important because they introduce the children to the idea of learning a rule and then applying it to different examples. This is a skill that is required in a variety of advanced comprehension activities.

Written Deductions Type 2
(Lessons 148–160)

The Written Deductions Type 2 track begins in lesson 148 and continues through lesson 160. The track contains one format. Shown here are the children's Worksheet activity from lesson 148 and the teacher presentation format.

The teacher-directed format is presented in three lessons—148, 149, and 150. The teacher takes the children through the steps in the deduction. In step 8, the teacher instructs the children to write the names of everyone who has a house with bugs.

Find out where the bugs are.

Here is the rule: Every white house has bugs.

Kim's house is brown.
Spot's house is white.
Ott's house is white.
Tim's house is red.
Mom's house is black.

Who has a house with bugs? _____ _____

Worksheet 148

Written deductions

a. (Pass out Worksheet 148 to each child.)
b. (Hold up side 1 of your worksheet and touch the sentence above the box in the deductions exercise.)
c. Everybody, touch this sentence on your worksheet. ✔
d. I'm going to call on individual children to read a sentence. Everybody, follow along.

1. (Call on a child.) Read the sentence above the box. *Find out where the bugs are.*
 • Everybody, what do you have to find out? (Signal.) *Where the bugs are.*

2. (Call on a child.) Read the sentence in the box. *Here is the rule: Every white house has bugs.*
 • Everybody, what's the rule? (Signal.) *Every white house has bugs.*
 • You need that rule to find out where the bugs are.

3. (Call on a child.) Read the first sentence below the box. *Kim's house is brown.*
 • Everybody, is Kim's house white? (Signal.) *No.*
 • And where are the bugs? (Signal.) *In every white house.*
 • So we don't know if Kim's house has bugs.

4. (Call on a child.) Read the next sentence. *Spot's house is white.*
 • Everybody, is Spot's house white? (Signal.) *Yes.*
 • And where are the bugs? (Signal.) *In every white house.*
 • So does Spot's house have bugs? (Signal.) *Yes.* Yes, Spot's house has bugs.

5. (Call on a child.) Read the next sentence. *Ott's house is white.*
 • Everybody, is Ott's house white? *Yes.* And where are the bugs? (Signal.) *In every white house.*
 • So does Ott's house have bugs? (Signal.) *Yes.* Yes, Ott's house has bugs.

6. (Call on a child.) Read the next sentence. *Tim's house is red.*
 • Everybody, is Tim's house white? (Signal.) *No.*
 • And where are the bugs? (Signal.) *In every white house.*
 • So we don't know if Tim's house has bugs.

7. (Call on a child.) Read the next sentence. *Mom's house is black.*
 • Everybody, is Mom's house white? (Signal.) *No.*
 • And where are the bugs? (Signal.) *In every white house.*
 • So we don't know if Mom's house has bugs.

8. (Call on a child.) Read the last sentence. *Who has a house with bugs?*
 • Everybody, what do you have to tell? (Signal.) *Who has a house with bugs.*
 • Write in the blanks the names of everyone who has a house with bugs. ✔

Lesson 148

Corrections

Expect the children to make mistakes in step 8. Typically, children omit some of the names of people who have a house with bugs.

To correct:

1. Have children say the rule about where the bugs are.

2. Have them read each sentence below the box and make a circle after it if there are bugs in the house.

3. After the children have circled every appropriate sentence, tell them: Look at each sentence with a circle after it and find the name of the person who owns that house. Then write the name of that person on the line in the item.

If children are firmed on the procedures during lessons 148 through 150, they probably will have no trouble working the remaining items in the track without supervision and without making mistakes.

Story-Items Review
(Lessons 101–147)

The Story-Items-Review track begins in lesson 101 and continues through lesson 147. The track contains one format.

The first story-items-review exercise in lesson 101 refers to a story that was read in lesson 91.

★★★★★★★★★★★★★★★★★★★★★★★★★★★★★★★★★★★★★

1. Did Sid tap the oak tree or tape the oak tree?

_____ the oak tree

2. Who told Sid, "I will teach you to read"?

_____

3. Did Sid become good at reading? _____

Worksheet 101

EXERCISE 7

Children read and do story-items review

a. (Pass out Worksheet 101 to each child.)
b. (Hold up side 1 of your worksheet and point to the row of stars below story item 4.)
c. Everybody, touch this row of stars on your worksheet. ✔
d. The items below the stars are about an old story. You didn't read that story today.
e. Everybody, get ready to read item 1. First word. ✔
• Get ready. (Tap for each word as the children read:) *Did Sid tap the oak tree or tape the oak tree?*
f. What's the answer to item 1? (Signal.) *Tap the oak tree.* Yes, **tap the oak tree.**
g. Everybody, write the answer in the blank. ✔
h. Read item 2 to yourself and raise your hand when you know the answer.
i. (When all the hands are raised, say:) Everybody, what's the answer to item 2? (Signal.) *The boss.*
j. Everybody, write the answer in the blank. ✔
k. Everybody, you'll do the other item later.

Lesson 101

Corrections

• If the children have trouble answering the question in step *f,* tell them the answer and structure the other items. (Have the children read the question and then answer it.)

• When you check the children's independent work and find that they cannot remember the answers to the review items, you can refer them to the appropriate Storybook page, which you will find noted in the Answer Key.

Note: From lesson 123 through lesson 147, the first exercise on side 2 of the Worksheet is the story-items review. There are no longer stars on the Worksheet.

Story Items (Lessons 121–160)

In lesson 121 (the lesson following the end of the Following-Instructions track), the story items incorporate directions of the form that has been in the following-instructions activities. The teacher presentation and the story items from lesson 121 are shown in the next column.

Practice the format before presenting it to the children. The format appears in two lessons—121 and 122. It is a good idea to monitor the children as they work the items. If they make mistakes, refer them to the instructions that appear in the box for the item they are working. Tell them to read the instructions and then work the item again.

A major objective of the story items is to give the children a great deal of practice in following written directions. The more facile they become in following them, the less trouble they will have reading for new information in later grades.

Make a line under the answer.

1. Carla was _____ from Ott's school book.
          reading   sitting   laughing

Fill in the blanks.

2. Carla said, "Ib, bub, ib, bub, ib, bub, bibby. Bome, _____ ,

   _____ . I want to go _____ , _____ ,

   _____ ."

3. Who said, "That is too much to remember"? _____

Circle the answer.

4. Who sent Carla home?
         an old genie   Carla   Ott

Fill in the blanks.

5. Did Ott go to Carla's home? _____

6. Who said, "I better call for help"? _____

Worksheet 121

Following instructions

a. (Pass out Worksheet 121 to each child.)

b. (Hold up side 1 of your worksheet and point to the story-items exercise.)

c. Everybody, touch item 1. ✔

d. Everybody, touch the instructions in the box above item 1. ✔

- Those instructions tell you how to work item 1. (Call on a child.) Read the instructions in the box. *Make a line under the answer.*

e. Everybody, what are you going to do to answer item 1? (Signal.) *Make a line under the answer.*

f. Everybody, touch the instructions in the box above item 2. ✔

- Those instructions tell you how to work items 2 and 3. (Call on a child.) Read the instructions in the box. *Fill in the blanks.*

g. Everybody, are you going to circle the answers? (Signal.) *No.*

- Are you going to make a line under the answers? (Signal.) *No.*

h. What are you going to do to work items 2 and 3? (Signal.) *Fill in the blanks.*

i. Everybody, touch the instructions in the box above item 4. ✔

- Those instructions tell you how to work item 4. (Call on a child.) Read the instructions in the box. *Circle the answer.*

j. Everybody, are you going to make a line under the answer? (Signal.) *No.*

- Are you going to fill in the blanks? (Signal.) *No.*

k. What are you going to do to work item 4? (Signal.) *Circle the answer.*

l. Everybody, touch the instructions in the box above item 5. ✔

- Those instructions tell you how to work items 5 and 6. (Call on a child.) Read the instructions in the box. *Fill in the blanks.*

m. Everybody, are you going to make a line under the answers? (Signal.) *No.*

- Are you going to circle the answers? (Signal.) *No.*

n. What are you going to do to work items 5 and 6? (Signal.) *Fill in the blanks.*

o. You'll work the items later. Remember to follow the instructions that go with each item.

Lesson 121

Reading Comprehension, Factual-Information Passages

(Lessons 132–160)

In lesson 132, the first "factual-information" reading-comprehension selection is introduced. These selections continue through lesson 160.

In many of the reading-comprehension passages from lessons 132 to 160, new science and social science information is introduced. Children apply some facts to passages in later lessons. In lesson 142, for example, children learn that the body of any insect has three parts. The rule is reviewed and children apply the rule in lesson 145. In that selection they are also taught more information about insects.

The children apply the skills they have learned in deductions exercises to these passages. Shown below are the teacher's directions and the comprehension selection for lesson 132.

EXERCISE 8

Reading comprehension

a. (Pass out Worksheet 132 to each child.)
b. Everybody, turn to side 2 of your worksheet. ✔
c. (Point to the story on side 2 of your worksheet.) Everybody, find this story on your worksheet. ✔
d. Today you're going to read a passage that tells about eggs. The pictures next to the passage show some of the animals that you'll read about.
e. Everybody, touch the chicken. ✔
f. Everybody, touch the snake. ✔
g. (Repeat step f for ant, turtle, fish, alligator.)
h. (Repeat steps e, f, and g until firm.)
i. I'll read the passage. Everybody, follow along. (Read the passage to the children. Check that they are following along as you read.)
j. When you do your independent work, read the passage to yourself. Then answer the questions.

Lesson 132

Chickens are not the only animals that lay eggs. A chicken is a bird, and all birds lay eggs. So do snakes and alligators. Turtles and fish also lay eggs. Did you know that ants and other bugs lay eggs? The egg holds the baby animal. A baby turtle comes out of an egg. And a baby snake comes out of an egg. Baby chickens come from the kind of eggs that you eat.

| Make a box under the answer. |
1. Are chickens the only animals that lay eggs?   Yes   No

| Make a line over the answer. |
2. All _____ lay eggs.   rabbits   birds   monkeys

| Fill in the blank. |
3. What does an egg hold? a baby _____

| Circle the answer. |
4. What is the best title for this story?
   Chickens Lay Eggs   Animals That Lay Eggs   The Baby Snake

Worksheet 132

Critical Behaviors

Check to see that the children can identify the pictures of the animals in steps e through g. For many children, this selection is the first science information they have read.

Read the passage to the children as they follow along. (Read at the same rate as you do when you read the stories. See page 74.) Starting at lesson 151 you do not read the passage. The children do all the activities independently during their seatwork.

Attend carefully to their workbook answers. Take the time to correct and firm.

Corrections

The most frequent type of mistake the children make is that of not remembering the information in the story. The children may either write down nonsense answers or go on to something else. Correct in the following way:

1. Have the children read the item aloud.

2. Say: What's the answer?

3. If they are unable to answer the question, say: That's a hard question, but you can find the answer if you read the story again.

4. Have the children read a sentence at a time. After each sentence, present the item that was missed and ask if the sentence gives the answer to the item.

Examples:

- If the children miss item 1 ("Are chickens the only animals that lay eggs?"), have the children read the first sentence; then ask: Does that sentence answer this question: "Are chickens the only animals that lay eggs?"

- If the children miss item 2 (All _____ lay eggs"), ask this question after the children read the first sentence and again after they read the second sentence: Does that sentence tell you that all somethings lay eggs? . . . What are those somethings?

You will probably need to use this firming procedure with lower-performing children.

PRACTICE the procedure with each of the four questions in the reading comprehension exercise from lesson 132.

APPENDIX

SAMPLE LESSONS

Lessons 11 and 105 and their corresponding Storybook and Workbook materials are reproduced here in their entirety so that you can practice the skills discussed in this guide before presenting Reading Mastery to your students. Spelling Lessons 11 and 105 appear starting on page 113. Spelling lessons should be presented *after* reading lessons.

Some children begin the program with this lesson. (See the placement section of your Teacher's Guide.)

SOUNDS

EXERCISE 1

Sounds firm-up

a. (Point to the sounds.) Tell me these sounds.

b. When I touch it, you say it. Keep on saying it as long as I touch it.

c. (Point to each sound.) Get ready. (Touch the sound.) (The children say the sound.) (Lift your finger.)

To Correct

1. (Immediately say the correct sound as you continue to touch it. Lift your finger.)
2. Say it with me. (Touch sound and say it with children.)
   • (Lift your finger.)
3. Again. (Repeat until firm.)
4. All by yourselves. Get ready. (Touch the sound.) (The children say the sound.)

d. (Repeat problem sounds until the children can correctly identify all sounds in order.)

Individual test

(Call on several children to identify one or more sounds.)

ā   e   er

wh   th   ē

y   sh   ch

p   h   g

READING VOCABULARY

Do not touch small letters.

Get ready to read all the words on this page without making a mistake.

To Correct

(Have the children sound out and tell what word.)

where

Sound out first

EXERCISE 2

a. (Touch the ball for **where.**) Sound it out. Get ready. (Quickly touch under **wh, e, r** as the children say:) *wwweeerrr.*
b. What word? (Signal.) *Where.* Yes, **where.**
c. (Repeat exercise until firm.)

there

Sound out first

EXERCISE 3

a. (Touch the ball for **there.**) Sound it out. Get ready. (Quickly touch under **th, e, r** as the children say:) *thththeeerrr.*
b. What word? (Signal.) *There.* Yes, **there.**
c. (Repeat exercise until firm.)

ar

EXERCISE 4

ar

a. (Point to **ar.**) When these letters are together, they usually say (pause) **are.** What do these letters say? (Signal.) *Are.* Yes, **are.**
b. (Repeat *a* until firm.)

arf

EXERCISE 5

ar words

a. (Point to **ar** in **arf.**) What do these letters say? (Signal.) *Are.* Yes, **are.**
b. (Touch the ball for **arf.**) Read this word the fast way. Get ready. (Signal.) *Arf.* Yes, **arf.**
c. (Repeat *a* and *b* for **barking.**)

barking

shark

EXERCISE 6

Read **ar** word the fast way

a. (Touch the ball for **shark.**) Read this word the fast way. (Pause two seconds.) Get ready. (Signal.) *Shark.* Yes, **shark.**
b. (Point to **ar** in **shark.**) Everybody, what do these letters say? (Signal.) *Are.* Yes, **are.**
c. (Touch the ball for **shark.**) Sound it out. Get ready. (Quickly touch under **sh, ar, k** as the children say:) *shshshark.*
d. What word? (Signal.) *Shark.* Yes, **shark.**
e. (Repeat *c* and *d* until firm.)

other

EXERCISE 7

Sound out first

a. (Touch the ball for **other.**) Sound it out. Get ready. (Quickly touch under **o, th, er** as the children say:) *ooooththerrr.*
b. What word? (Signal.) *Other.* Yes, **other.**
c. (Repeat exercise until firm.)

Individual test

(Repeat any troublesome words.)

(Call on individual children. Each child reads a different word.)

līked

help

Do not touch small letters.

Get ready to read all the words on this page without making a mistake.

To Correct

(Have the children sound out and tell what word.)

yelled

swam

EXERCISE 9
Read the fast way first

a. (Touch the ball for **help.**) Read this word the fast way. (Pause two seconds.) Get ready. (Signal.) *Help.* Yes, **help.**

b. (Return to the ball.) Sound it out. Get ready. (Quickly touch under **h, e, l, p** as the children say:) *heeelllp.*

c. What word? (Signal.) *Help.* Yes, **help.**

d. (Repeat *b* and *c* until firm.)

e. (Repeat the exercise for **helped, after, līked, yelled, away,** and **swimming.**)

EXERCISE 8
Last part, first part

a. (Cover **s.** Point to **wam.**) Read this part of the word the fast way. (Pause two seconds.) Get ready. (Signal.) *Wam.* Yes, **wam.**

b. (Uncover **s.** Point to **s.**) First you say **sss.** (Move your finger quickly under **wam.**) Then you say (pause) **wam.**

c. (Touch the ball for **swam.**) Get ready. (Move to **s,** then quickly along the arrow.) *Ssswam.*

d. Say it fast. (Signal.) *Swam.*
• Yes, what word? (Signal.) *Swam.* Yes, **swam.**
• Good reading.

e. (Repeat *c* and *d* until firm.)

away

helped

after

swimming

(Repeat any troublesome words.)

Individual test

(Call on individual children. Each child reads a different word.)

11

Do not touch small letters.

Get ready to read all the words on this page without making a mistake.

To Correct
(Have the children sound out and tell what word.)

EXERCISE 10

Read the fast way

a. Read these words the fast way.

b. (Touch the ball for **another.** Pause two seconds.) Get ready. (Signal.) *Another.* Yes, **another.**

c. (Repeat *b* for **whȳ, when,** and **funny.**)

another

whȳ

when

funny

book

EXERCISE 11

Read the fast way first

a. (Touch the ball for **book.**) Read this word the fast way. (Pause two seconds.) Get ready. (Signal.) *Book.* Yes, **book.**

b. (Return to the ball.) Sound it out. Get ready. (Quickly touch under **b, oo, k** as the children say:) *boooök.*

c. What word? (Signal.) *Book.* Yes, **book.**

d. (Repeat *b* and *c* until firm.)

took

EXERCISE 12

Read the fast way first

a. (Touch the ball for **took.**) Read this word the fast way. (Pause two seconds.) Get ready. (Signal.) *Took.* Yes, **took.**

b. (Return to the ball.) Sound it out. Get ready. (Quickly touch under **t, oo, k** as the children say:) *toooök.*

c. What word? (Signal.) *Took.* Yes, **took.**

d. (Repeat *b* and *c* until firm.)

EXERCISE 13

Read the fast way

a. Read these words the fast way.

b. (Touch the ball for **looked.** Pause two seconds.) Get ready. (Signal.) *Looked.* Yes, **looked.**

c. (Repeat *b* for **cooked.**)

looked

cooked

Individual test

(Call on individual children to read a column of words from this lesson. If the column contains only one or two words, direct the child to read additional words from another column. Praise children who read all words with no errors.)

STORYBOOK

STORY 11

EXERCISE 14

First reading—title and three sentences

a. (Pass out Storybook 1.)

b. Everybody, open your reader to page 17. ✔

c. Everybody, touch the title. (Check to see that the children are touching under the first word of the title.)

d. I'll tap and you read each word in the title the fast way. Don't sound it out. Just tell me the word.

e. First word. ✔
• (Pause two seconds.) Get ready. (Tap.) *Arf.*

f. Next word. (Check to see that the children are touching under the next word. Pause two seconds.) Get ready. (Tap.) *The.*

g. (Repeat f for the remaining word in the title.)

h. Everybody, say the title. (Signal.) *Arf the shark.* Yes, **Arf the shark.**

i. Everybody, get ready to read this story the fast way.

j. First word. ✔
• (Pause two seconds.) Get ready. (Tap.) *Arf.*

k. Next word. ✔
• (Pause two seconds.) Get ready. (Tap.) *Was.*

l. (Repeat k for the remaining words in the first three sentences. Have the children reread the first three sentences until firm.)

EXERCISE 15

Remaining sentences

a. I'm going to call on individual children to read a sentence. Everybody, follow along and point to the words. If you hear a mistake, raise your hand.

b. (Call on a child.) Read the next sentence.

To Correct
word-identification errors
(**from**, for example)
1. That word is **from.** What word? *From.*
2. Go back to the beginning of the sentence and read the sentence again.

c. (Call on another child.) Read the next sentence.

d. (Repeat c for most of the remaining sentences in the story.)

e. (Occasionally have the group read a sentence. When the group is to read, say:) Everybody, read the next sentence. (Pause two seconds. Tap for each word in the sentence. Pause at least two seconds between taps.)

Note: Underlined and numbered statements in the following copy of story 11 refer to questions you are to ask the children in exercise 16.

arꞙ the shark[1]

arꞙ was a barking shark. arꞙ was a little shark, but shē had a big bark that māde the other fish swim awāy.[2]

a shark swam up to arꞙ and said, "you arₑ a shark. let's plāy."

arꞙ was happy. "arꞙ, arꞙ," shē said.[3] and the other shark swam far, far awāy. arꞙ was not happy now.[4]

another shark swam up to arꞙ. "you arₑ a shark," hē said. "let's plāy."

arꞙ was happy. "arꞙ, arꞙ," shē said. and the other shark swam far, far awāy. arꞙ was not happy now.

then a big, big fish that līked to ēat sharks swam up to the other sharks.[5]

"help, help," they yelled.[6] but the big fish was swimming after them very fast. stop[7]

EXERCISE 16

Second reading—sentences and questions

a. You're going to read the story again. This time I'm going to ask questions.

b. Starting with the first word of the title. ✔ Get ready. (Tap as the children read the title.)

c. (Call on a child.) Read the first sentence.

> **To Correct**
>
> word-identification errors (**from,** for example)
> 1. That word is **from.** What word? *From.*
> 2. Go back to the beginning of the sentence and read the sentence again.

d. (Call on another child.) Read the next sentence.

e. (Repeat *d* for most of the remaining sentences in the story.)

f. (Occasionally have the group read a sentence.)

g. (After each underlined sentence has been read, present each comprehension question specified below to the entire group.)

[1] What's this story about? (Signal.) *Arf the shark.*

[2] Who was Arf? (Signal.) *A little shark.*

[3] What did Arf say? Let's hear you say it like Arf said it. (Signal.) *Arf, arf.*

[4] Why wasn't she happy? (The children respond.)

[5] What did the big fish like to eat? (Signal.) *Sharks.*

• Let's see if the big fish eats any.

[6] Why did the sharks yell? (The children respond.)

[7] Is this the end of the story? (Signal.) *No.*

• Right. We stop now. We'll finish the story next time.

EXERCISE 17

Picture comprehension

a. Look at the picture.

b. (Ask these questions:)

1. Show me the shark you think is Arf. (The children respond.)

2. What does it look like Arf is doing? (The children respond.)

3. What is that big fish doing? (The children respond.)

4. What would you do if you were Arf? (Let the children comment for ten seconds. Then comment briefly.)

WORKSHEET 11

STORY ITEMS

EXERCISE 18

Read the story items

a. (Pass out Worksheet 11 to each child.)

b. (Hold up side 1 of your worksheet and point to the story-items exercise.) Everybody, you're going to read the items for the story you just read. You're going to circle the answers later.

c. (Touch the blank in item 1.) Here's where something is missing. When you get to this blank, say "**blank.**"

d. Get ready to read item 1 the fast way. First word. ✔

• Get ready. (Tap.) *Arf.*

e. Next word. ✔

• Get ready. (Tap.) *Was.*

f. (Repeat *e* for the remaining words in item 1.)

g. Tell me the answer. Arf was a barking . . . . (Signal.) *Shark.*

• What word goes in the blank? (Signal.) *Shark.* (The children are not to circle the answers now.)

h. (Repeat *d* through *g* for item 2.)

i. You're going to do these items later. Remember to circle the right answer for each item.

SENTENCE COPYING

EXERCISE 19

Read sentence to copy

a. (Point to the sentence **shē is in a car.**)

b. Here's the sentence you're going to write on the lines below. Everybody, touch this sentence on your worksheet. ✔

c. Get ready to read the words in this sentence the fast way. First word. ✔

• Get ready. (Tap for each word as the children read:) *She is in a car.*

d. (Have the children reread the sentence the fast way.)

e. (Point to the dotted words on the first line.) Later, you're going to trace the dotted words in this sentence. Then you're going to write these words on the other lines.

SOUND WRITING

EXERCISE 20

Identify sounds to be written

a. (Point to the sound-writing exercise.) Everybody, here are the sounds you're going to write today. I'll touch the sounds. You say them.

b. (Touch each sound.) (The children respond.)

c. (Repeat *b* until firm.)

d. You're going to write a sound on each bar. You'll write the sounds later.

READING COMPREHENSION

The children will need pencils.

EXERCISE 21

Read story, answer items

a. (Hold up side 2 of your worksheet and point to the word **reading.**) Everybody, touch this story on your worksheet. ✔

b. Reading the fast way. First word. ✔

• Get ready. (Tap.) *A.*

c. Next word. ✔

• Get ready. (Tap.) *Boy.*

d. (Repeat *c* for the remaining words in the story.)

e. (Hold up your worksheet. Touch the blank in item 1.) Everybody, here's where something is missing. When you get to this blank, say "**blank.**"

f. Reading item 1 the fast way. First word. ✔

• Get ready. (Tap.) *A.*

g. Next word. ✔

• Get ready. (Tap.) *Blank.*

h. (Repeat *g* for the remaining words in item 1.) (Children read *ate, cake.*)

i. Everybody, what word goes in the blank? (Signal.) *Boy.*

j. (Repeat *i* until firm.)

k. Look at the words under item 1 and get ready to touch the word that goes in the blank. (Pause.) Get ready. (Signal.) ✔

l. Circle the word **boy.** ✔

m. (Repeat *f* through *l* for item 2.)

11 PICTURE COMPREHENSION

EXERCISE 22

Write words for picture

Refer to sounds, not letter names, in missing words.

a. (Hold up side 2 of your worksheet and point to the first picture.) Look at this picture. Tell me what you see. (Accept reasonable responses.)

b. Everybody, who looks old? (Signal.) *The man.* Yes, this man is old.

c. Everybody, what is the man holding? (Signal.) *A rug.*
• Yes, he has a . . . . (Signal.) *Rug.*

d. (Repeat *b* and *c* until firm.)

e. (Point to the sound in the blank in item 1.) Something is missing. When you get to this, say "**blank.**" What will you say? (Signal.) *Blank.*

f. Everybody, touch item 1 next to the picture. ✔

g. Get ready to read item 1 the fast way. First word. ✔
• Get ready. (Tap.) *This.*

h. Next word. ✔
• Get ready. (Tap.) *Blank.*

i. (Repeat *h* for the remaining words in item 1.)

j. (Repeat *g* through *i* until firm.)

k. What word goes in the blank? (Signal.) *Man.*

l. I'll say the sounds in the word **man. mmm** (pause) **aaa** (pause) **nnn. mmm** (pause) **aaa** (pause) **nnn.**

m. Your turn. Say the sounds in **man.** Get ready. (Signal for each sound as the children say:) *mmm* (pause) *aaa* (pause) *nnn.*

n. (Repeat *l* and *m* until firm.)

o. Look at the blank in item 1. The **mmm** is already written in the blank. So what sounds are you going to write next? (Signal for each sound as the children say:) *aaa* (pause) *nnn.*
• (Repeat until firm.)

p. Everybody, write the missing sounds for **man.** ✔

q. (Repeat *g* through *p* for item 2.)

r. You'll do the items for the other picture later.

SUMMARY OF INDEPENDENT ACTIVITY

EXERCISE 23

a. (Hold up side 1 of Worksheet 11.)

b. Everybody, you're going to finish this worksheet on your own. (Tell the children when they will work the remaining items.)
• Let's go over the things you're going to do.

Story items

(Point to the story items exercise.) Remember to read the items and circle the answers that tell what happened in the story.

Sentence copying

(Point to the first line in the sentence-copying exercise.) Remember—you're going to trace the words in this sentence. Then you're going to write the sentence on the other lines.

Sound writing

(Point to the sound-writing exercise.) Remember to write a sound on each bar.

Picture comprehension

a. (Point to the second picture in the picture-comprehension exercise.) Everybody, you're going to look at this picture. Then you're going to read each item and write the missing words.

b. Remember—the first sound of each missing word is already written in the blank.

END OF LESSON 11

arf the shark

arf was a barking shark. arf was a little shark, but she had a big bark that māde the other fish swim awāy.

a shark swam up to arf and said, "you arₑ a shark. let's plāy."

arf was happy. "arf, arf," shē said. and the other shark swam far, far awāy. arf was not happy now.

another shark swam up to arf. "you arₑ a shark," hē said. "let's plāy."

arf was happy. "arf, arf," shē said. and the other shark

17

swam far, far awāy. arf was not happy now.

then a big, big fish that līked to ēat sharks swam up to the other sharks.

"help, help," they yelled. but the big fish was swimming after them very fast.

stop

18

Name _____   Worksheet 11   Side 1

stōry Items

1. arf was a barkin͞g ▦ _____ .
   ● card   ● shark   ● farm

2. a big ▦ _____ swam up to the other sharks.
   ● fish   ● fin   ● fan

shē is in a car.

she is in a car.

h _ _ _ _ _ _

w _ _ _ _ _ _

v _ _ _ _ _ _

n _ _ _ _ _ _

u _ _ _ _ _ _

m _ _ _ _ _ _

Worksheet 11   Side 2

rēadin͞g

a boy āte cāke.

hē got sick.

1. a ▦ _____ āte cāke.
   ● man   ● boy   ● girl

2. hē got ▦ _____ .
   ● sick   ● sad   ● wet

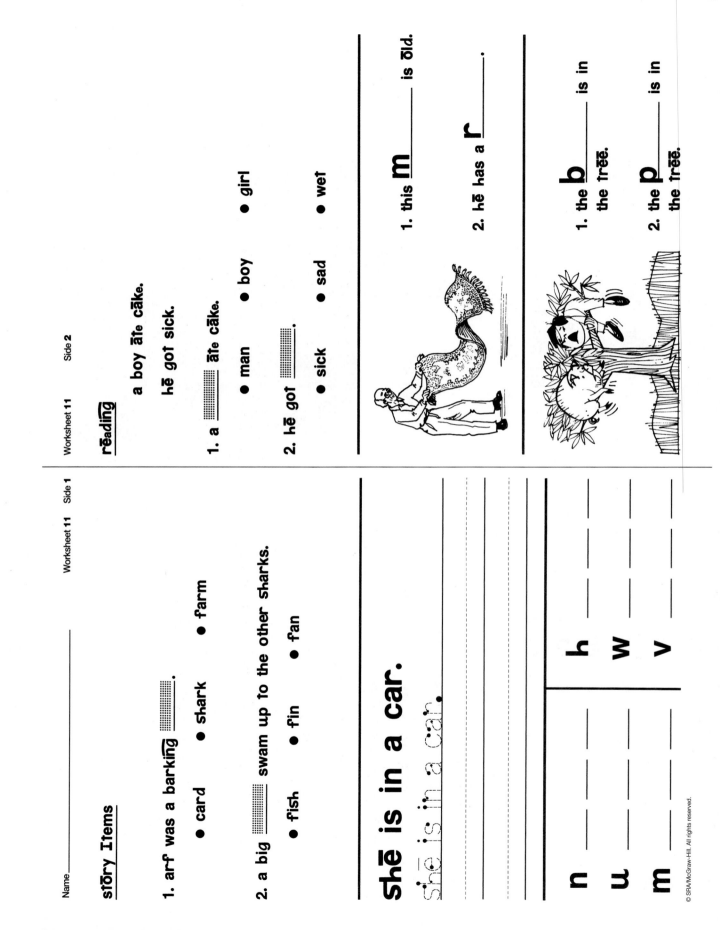

1. this **m** _____ is ōld.

2. hē has a **r** _____ .

1. the **b** _____ is in the trēē.

2. the **p** _____ is in the trēē.

(modified for practice)
READING VOCABULARY

EXERCISE 1

Teacher reads the words in red

a. I'll read each word in red. Then you'll spell each word.

b. (Touch the ball for **animal.**) My turn. (Slash as you say:) Animal. What word? (Signal.) *Animal.*

c. (Return to the ball.) Spell it. Get ready. (Tap under each letter as the children say:) *A-N-I-M-A-L.*

- What word did you spell? (Signal.) *Animal.*

d. (Repeat steps *b* and *c* for each word in red.)

e. Your turn to read all the words in this column.

f. (Touch the ball for **animal.** Pause.) Get ready. (Slash.) *Animal.*

g. (Repeat step *f* for each remaining word in the column.)

h. (Repeat steps *f* and *g* until firm.)

animal

tickle

roared

toad

howling

leave

turn

EXERCISE 2

Read the fast way

a. You're going to read all the words in this column the fast way.

b. (Touch the ball for **spell.** Pause.) Get ready. (Slash.) *Spell.*

c. (Repeat step *b* until firm.)

d. (Repeat steps *b* and *c* for each remaining word in the column.)

e. (Repeat the column until the children read all the words in order without making mistakes.)

To Correct
word-identification errors (**note**, for example)

1. That word is **note.** What word? (Signal.) *Note.*
2. Spell **note.** Get ready. Tap under each letter. *N-o-t-e.*
3. What word did you spell? (Signal.) *Note.*
4. Repeat 2 and 3 until firm.
5. (Return to the first word in the column and present all words in order.) **Starting over.**

spell

note

magic

Castle

don't

stream

bead

Criterion

(If the children make any mistakes in the column, say:) Do this column again without making any mistakes. (Repeat the column.)

(If the children make no mistakes in the column, say:) Good reading. You made no mistakes in this column. (Proceed to the next column.)

Criterion

(If the children make any mistakes in the column, say:) Do this column again without making any mistakes. (Repeat the column.)

(If the children make no mistakes in the column, say:) Good reading. You made no mistakes in this column. (Proceed to the next column.)

EXERCISE 3

Words with underlined parts

a. First you're going to read the underlined part of each word in this column. Then you're going to read the whole word.

b. (Touch the ball for **stays.**) Read the underlined part. Get ready. (Tap the ball.) *Stays.*

• Read the whole word. (Pause.) Get ready. (Slash.) *Stays.*

c. (Repeat step b until firm.)

d. (Repeat steps b and c for each remaining word in the column.)

e. (Repeat the column until children read all the words in order without making a mistake.)

stays
meanest
turned
anybody
really
walls
holding

EXERCISE 4

Children spell, then read

a. First you're going to spell each word. Then you're going to read that word the fast way.

b. (Touch the ball for **Who.**) Spell it. Get ready. (Tap under each letter as the children say:) *W-H-O.*

• (Return to the ball.) Read it. Get ready. (Slash.) *Who.*

c. (Repeat step b for each remaining word in the column.)

d. (Repeat steps b and c until firm.)

Who
made
floated
watched
long
robed
robbed

Individual test

a. (Call on individual children to read one column of words from the lesson.)

b. (Praise children who read all words with no errors.)

STORY 105

EXERCISE 5

Reading—decoding

a. (Pass out Storybook 2.)

b. Everybody, open your reader to page 60.

c. Remember, if the group reads all the way to the red 5 without making more than five errors, we can go on.

d. Everybody, touch the title of the story. ✔

e. If you hear a mistake, raise your hand. Remember, children who do not have their place lose their turn. (Call on individual children to read two or three sentences. Do not ask comprehension questions. Tally all errors.)

To Correct

word-identification errors (**from,** for example)
1. That word is **from.** What word? *From.*
2. Go back to the beginning of the sentence and read the sentence again.

f. (If the children make more than five errors before they reach the red 5: when they reach the 5 return to the beginning of the story and have the children reread to the 5. Do not ask comprehension questions. Repeat step *f* until firm, and then go on to step *g.*)

g. (When the children read to the red 5 without making more than five errors: read the story to the children from the beginning to the 5. Ask the specified comprehension questions. When you reach the 5, call on individual children to continue reading the story. Have each child read two or three sentences.
Ask the specified comprehension questions.)

Boo Goes to the Castle[1]

The five mean ghosts had made Boo leave the old house. When Boo was walking to town, he found a talking frog. The frog was near a stream. But the frog was not really a frog. It was a king. A monster had cast a spell on the king and turned him into a frog.[2]

"I will help you," Boo said. "Just tell me where the monster stays."

The frog said, "The monster is in my castle. That castle is on the other side of town."[3]

"You wait here," Boo said. "I will be back."

Boo floated up into the sky. He floated over the town like a bird. Soon he came to the castle ★ on the other side of town.[4] When he floated near the castle, the hounds began to howl.[5] Boo floated to the top of the wall that went around the castle. ⑤ The hounds were howling and howling.

Then the door to the castle opened and out came the meanest-looking monster Boo had ever seen. That monster roared, "Who is out here? Who is making my hounds howl?"[6]

---

[1] What's going to happen in this story? (Signal.) *Boo will go to the castle.*

[2] How did the king get to be a frog? (The children respond.) Yes, a monster cast a spell on the frog.

[3] Where does the monster stay? (The children respond.)
- Whose castle is it? (The children respond.)
- Where is that castle? (Signal.) *On the other side of town.*

[4] How did Boo get there? (The children respond.) Yes, he floated in the sky like a bird.

[5] Tell me how those hounds sounded. (The children respond.)

[6] Who is talking? (Signal.) *The monster.*
- Why are the hounds howling? (The children respond.)

105

Boo did not say a thing. He just watched the monster.

The monster roared, "If you don't leave, I'll get you. I'll turn you into a frog or a toad."[7]

When the monster went back into the castle, Boo floated from the wall. He found a window and went inside the castle. He could see the monster. Boo said to himself, "That monster is really mean."[8]

The monster was holding a gold rod. She was saying, "As long as I have this magic rod, I can cast a spell over anybody. I can turn anybody into a frog or a toad."[9]

Boo said to himself, "I must get that magic rod from the monster."[10]

Stop

INDEPENDENT ACTIVITIES

EXERCISE 7

Summary of independent activities

a. (Pass out Worksheet 105 to each child.)

b. Everybody, now you'll do your worksheet. Remember to do all parts of the worksheet and to read all the parts carefully.

INDIVIDUAL CHECKOUT

EXERCISE 8

2-minute individual fluency checkout: rate/accuracy

a. As you are doing your worksheet, I'll call on children one at a time to read to the star. Remember, you get two stars on the chart if you read to the star in less than two minutes and make no more than four errors.

b. (Call on each child. Tell the child:) Read to the star very carefully. Start with the title. Go. (Time the child. Tell the child any words the child misses. Stop the child as soon as the child makes the fifth error or exceeds the time limit.)

c. (If the child meets the rate-accuracy criterion, record two stars on your chart for lesson 105. Congratulate the child. Give children who do not earn two stars a chance to read to the star again before the next lesson is presented.)

120 words/**2 min** = 60 wpm **[4 errors]**

END OF LESSON 105

---

7   What did the monster say she would do? (Signal.) *Turn Boo into a frog or a toad.*
8   Where is Boo? (Signal.) *Inside the castle.*
9   What does the monster use to cast her spells? (Signal.) *A magic rod.*
10   What does Boo want to get? (Signal.) *The magic rod.*
• Next time we'll see if he gets the magic rod.

EXERCISE 6

Picture comprehension

a. Look at the picture.

b. (Ask these questions:)
1. Who is that mean-looking thing? (Signal.) *The monster.*
   • That's the meanest monster I've ever seen. Are there really monsters like that? (The children respond.)
2. Does Boo look afraid? (Signal.) *Yes.*
3. What's that building the monster lives in? (Signal.) *A castle.*
4. What are the dogs doing? (Signal.) *Howling.*
5. Is it daytime or nighttime in this picture? (Signal.) *Nighttime.*
   • How do you know? (The children respond.)

Boo Goes to the Castle

The five mean ghosts had made Boo leave the old house. When Boo was walking to town, he found a talking frog. The frog was not really a frog. It was a king. A monster had cast a spell on the king and turned him into a frog.

"I will help you," Boo said. "Just tell me where the monster stays."

The frog said, "The monster is in my castle. That castle is on the other side of town."

"You wait here," Boo said. "I will be back."

Boo floated up into the sky. He floated over the town like a bird. Soon he came to the castle ★ on the other side of town. When he floated near the castle, the hounds began to howl. Boo floated to the

60

top of the wall that went around the castle.⑤ The hounds were howling and howling.

Then the door to the castle opened and out came the meanest-looking monster Boo had ever seen. That monster roared, "Who is out here? Who is making my hounds howl?"

Boo did not say a thing. He just watched the monster.

The monster roared, "If you don't leave, I'll get you. I'll turn you into a frog or a toad."

When the monster went back into the castle, Boo floated from the wall. He found a window and went inside the castle. He could see the monster. Boo said to himself, "That monster is really mean."

The monster was holding a gold rod. She was saying, "As long as I have this

61

magic rod, I can cast a spell over anybody. I can turn anybody into a frog or a toad."

Boo said to himself, "I must get that magic rod from the monster."

Stop

62

1. Who said, "I will help you"? _____

2. Who said, "The monster is in my castle"? _____

3. Boo floated over the _____.

　　town　　lake　　sky　　moon

4. When Boo floated near the castle, the _____ began to howl.

　　ghosts　　hounds　　cows　　monster

5. Who said, "I'll turn you into a frog or a toad"? the _____

　　king　　ghost　　monster　　hound

6. The monster was holding a gold _____ .

　　hat　　mouse　　rod　　toad

7. Who said, "I must get that magic rod from the monster"? a _____

8. What is the title of this story? _____

★★★★★★★★★★★★★★★★★★★★★★★★★★★★★★★★★★

1. Who worked for the boss? _____

2. Did Sid send a cone to the farm or a con to the farm? a _____

3. Did the note tell Sid to plant seeds on the slope or in the slop? _____

The snow on the hill looks white.

1. Make an r over the word snow.
2. Circle the word white.
3. Make a box around the words that tell where the snow is.

　　　There was an elephant that liked to jump. Everybody tried to get him to stop jumping. He was making a mess. One day a tiger said, "I will stop his jumping." The tiger made a big hole in the ground. He put grass over the hole. Then he told the elephant to jump on that grass. When the elephant jumped, he fell into the hole. Fifty bugs tickled him and tickled him. The elephant said he would not jump again. Now everybody is happy.

1. Who liked to jump? _____

2. The tiger made a h_____ in the ground.

3. Fifty _____ tickled the elephant.

Pam has all of the little kites.

Circle every kite that Pam has.

INDEPENDENT READERS

Reading Mastery, Grade 1: Independent Readers. Both Library sets consist of six copies each of five titles. These illustrated books provide children with an opportunity to practice their reading skills as they progress through *Reading Mastery.* The text of each story consists of words that children have learned by the lesson the book is introduced.

The tables below show the lesson to be completed before introducing children to each title.

For *Reading Mastery,* Grade 1

Set 1 Titles	Reading Mastery Classic Use after lesson	
	Grade 1	Fast Cycle
The Big Gold Ring	10	81
The Boy Who Yelled "Wolf"	40	90
The Bad Wind and the 3 Clouds	70	106
Bill Makes a Mountain	100	126
The Hidden Door	125	150

For *Reading Mastery,* Grade 1

Set 2 Titles	Reading Mastery Classic Use after lesson	
	Grade 1	Fast Cycle
The Pet Home	10	81
Fred and the Pig	40	90
The Jumping Box	70	106
The Goat Who Ate the Radio	100	126
Steg and the Monster	125	150

INDEPENDENT READING LIST

The following books are suggested for independent student reading. Present the books to your children at any time after they have completed the specified lessons in *Reading Mastery,* Grade 1.

Lesson

1 **Have You Seen My Cat?** Eric Carle, 94 words. When a boy's cat disappears, his search leads him to many other cats, but none are his cat. In the end, a man and woman tell him where his cat is.

20 **We Hide, You Seek.** Jose Aruego & Ariane Dewey. 29 words. A nearsighted rhino who is playing a game of hide-and-seek accidentally finds the other animals who are hiding by stepping on them or startling them. Then the rhino hides in a unique hiding place. The other animals cannot find the rhino because the rhino hides in a group of other rhinos.

36 **I Love You, Dear Dragon.** 275 words. A dragon accompanies a boy to school, makes valentines with him, and sits with him when the boy's father reads stories. The boy loves dear dragon.

41 **If All the Seas Were One Sea.** Janina Domanska, 89 words. The story suggests what would happen if all trees became one tree, if all axes were made into one ax, and if all people were combined to make one person. If all the seas were one sea, what a great sea that would be.

46 **Blue Sea.** Robert Kalan, 75 words. Bigger fish chase smaller fish through holes. The only fish that gets through the smallest hole is the littlest fish.

58 **Green Eggs & Ham.** Dr. Seuss. 812 words. Sam-I-Am repeatedly offers a character wearing a black hat, green eggs and ham, but the character refuses to eat them until the end of the story. The character then discovers that green eggs and ham are good.

60 **Go, Dog, Go!** Philip D. Eastman, 518 words. Dogs of various shapes, colors, and sizes have a series of adventures in cars, on boats, and in trees.

61 **The Farmer in the Dell.** The lyrics from the familiar song are combined with pictures.

62 **Mine's the Best.** Crosby N. Bonsall. 107 words. Two boys have balloons at the beach. Each boy argues that his balloon is the best. As the boys argue, the balloons deflate. Then somebody comes along the beach with bundles of fully-inflated balloons.

70 **The Carrot Seed.** Ruth Krauss. 101 words. A boy plants a carrot seed. Members of his family tell the boy that the seed will not grow. But it does grow—into a gigantic carrot.

73 **Whose Mouse Are You?** Robert Kraus. 108 words. A lonely mouse liberates its mother from inside a cat, its father from inside a trap, and its sister from a mountaintop. After these heroic efforts, the mouse has a family again, including something new—a baby brother mouse.

74 **The Friend.** John Burningham, 47 words. A boy tells about his relationship with his friend Arthur. The boys have a lot of fun playing, but when they fight, Arthur goes home and the boy finds interim friends to play with. Arthur remains the best friend, however.

75 **Three Little Kittens Lost Their Mittens.** Three kittens each lose mittens. The mother cat tells the kittens that they will have no pie until they have found their mittens, which are seen in the pictures.

76 **Brown Bear, Brown Bear, What Do You See?** Bill Martin, Jr. 258 words. Brown Bear sees an animal that is looking at Brown Bear. That animal in turn sees another animal who is looking at that animal. The chain continues through nine animals.

79 **Home For a Bunny.** Margaret Wise Brown, 357 words. A bunny looks for a home in a lot of places before finding the right home, a hole occupied by another bunny.

80 **Who Took the Farmer's Hat?** Joan L. Nodset. 350 words. The wind carries the farmer's old brown hat on a journey that ends when the hat becomes a bird's nest. The farmer follows the hat's journey, but when he sees that it is being used as a nest, he decides to buy a new brown hat.

81 **A Kiss For Little Bear.** Else H. Minarik. 303 words. Grandmother Bear is delighted with the picture Little Bear has made for her and sends a kiss back to him by pony express—through several animals. The kiss almost gets lost.

85 **Hop on Pop.** Dr. Seuss. 383 words. Some characters have adventures sitting on hats, sitting on a cactus, and playing ball on a wall. Others find out that they should not hop on Pop.

READING VOCABULARY WORD LIST

This list includes only those words that are introduced in Reading Vocabulary. Additional words are used in the stories and Worksheets. The number following each word refers to the lesson in which the word first appears in Reading Vocabulary.

able   115
about   48
across   118
afraid   50
after   11
again   63
agreed   122
ahead   140
air   116
Alaska   126
alive   137
all   31
alligator   112
almost   45
alone   114
along   108
already   130
also   38
always   38
America   143
and   94
angry   155
animal   105
animals   141
Ann   95
another   10
answer   83
answered   25
any   40
anybody   88
anyhow   109
anyone   53
anything   67
anywhere   156
appear   111
appeared   117
appears   115
apple   112

are   1
arf   10
ark   10
arm   5
arms   102
around   50
arrows   160
art   7
as   92
ask   20
asked   21
asleep   140
at   4
ate   3
away   6

babies   154
baby   88
back   24
bag   29
bags   27
bake   21
baked   22
bakes   21
bald   102
ball   30
balls   43
banana   149
bananas   151
band   144
bank   16
banking   115
bar   1
barge   158
bark   10
barked   10
barking   11
barn   3
bath   10

bay   159
beach   113
bead   105
bean   102
beans   67
bear   67
beat   114
became   66
because   27
become   100
been   55
bees   142
before   52
began   64
begin   96
behind   53
being   116
believe   118
believed   119
belong   126
bending   61
bent   34
best   16
bet   37
better   12
bide   114
big   6
bigger   54
biggest   104
bike   17
bikes   19
bin   109
bird   27
bit   61
bite   61
biter   137
bites   108
biting   125
bitter   137
black   132
blanks   120
blew   155
blow   26
blowing   64
blushed   116
bode   106
body   142

bones   22
bong   136
boo   103
book   10
books   12
boomed   144
boss   90
bottles   112
bottom   55
bout   46
bowl   101
box   34
boy   14
boys   96
brag   158
branch   132
breathe   159
bring   128
bringing   127
broke   83
broken   119
broom   23
brother   20
brothers   28
brown   147
brush   25
bug   34
bumpy   111
bunch   114
bushes   141
bust   114
but   19
buttons   28
buy   29
buying   81

cake   21
call   33
called   36
calling   37
cam   56
came   7
can   6
candy   37
cane   55
caned   91
canes   119

canned   91
canner   94
cannot   28
cans   119
can't   36
cap   54
cape   54
caped   107
capped   107
car   1
card   21
care   77
careful   54
Carl   132
Carla   114
Carmen   48
carry   88
cars   42
cart   2
Casey   142
cash   97
cast   104
castle   104
casts   110
cave   134
caw   132
chair   142
charm   2
chase   130
chasing   138
check   73
cheek   87
cheeks   134
cheer   42
cheered   42
cheering   42
cheese   94
chicken   131
children   48
chill   142
China   126
chop   150
chunk   132
chunks   37
circle   17
city   115
clap   1

clapped 126
class 124
clean 56
clock 127
close 80
closed 80
closer 118
clothes 145
cloud 45
clouds 50
coat 134
cold 30
colder 79
color 136
come 16
coming 52
con 80
cone 80
coned 114
cones 133
conned 80
cons 133
contest 159
continued 82
cooked 11
cookie 138
cool 80
cop 6
cope 109
copper 118
corner 128
could 38
couldn't 41
counted 68
counter 68
cow 14
crackers 144
crash 85
crashed 85
cream 80
creek 14
cried 19
croak 137
crooks 71
cross 54
crossed 140
crow 132

crown 145
crump 146
cry 17
crying 14

Dan 95
dance 146
dancing 148
dare 122
dark 83
darker 64
darn 159
dart 108
darted 160
day 82
dear 153
deep 79
deepest 146
dental 129
did 4
didn't 3
die 144
dig 6
dim 31
dime 22
dimes 83
dimmed 113
dimmer 113
diner 89
dinner 41
dirty 56
disappear 112
disappeared 152
disappears 118
dish 73
dive 85
do 4
docks 159
does 56
doesn't 109
dog 6
doing 25
dollars 128
done 78
Don's 26
don't 3
door 53

dragging 128
drank 131
dream 35
dreaming 35
dress 106
dressed 145
dresses 106
drink 80
drive 129
drop 26
dropped 26
dropping 27
drops 27
dry 131
duckling 100
dug 6
dumped 92
dusty 139

each 26
eagle 22
early 95
ears 79
easiest 156
east 127
easy 73
eat 101
eaten 151
eating 107
egg 100
eight 153
elephant 39
elf 54
Ellen's 131
else 76
even 4
ever 38
Everest 158
every 2
everybody 78
everything 68
eye 141
eyes 51

face 116
faced 144
fact 118

fall 31
falling 43
falls 39
false 129
far 1
farm 2
farmer 29
farms 30
fast 14
faster 15
fastest 138
fat 33
fate 62
father 51
fear 106
feathers 131
feel 110
fell 15
felt 41
few 120
fifty 67
fight 122
figure 156
filed 151
filled 117
fin 43
finally 159
find 24
finding 75
fine 23
fingers 124
finish 140
fire 65
fires 66
first 66
fish 20
five 63
fix 59
fixed 88
fixes 94
flame 134
flash 108
flew 108
flies 114
flip 120
flipped 120
flipping 121

float 65
floated 66
floating 108
flock 137
floor 34
flow 118
flowed 122
flower 109
fly 14
flying 17
folded 115
followed 70
fool 94
football 37
footprint 133
for 3
forest 65
forget 115
forgot 145
formed 118
forward 148
found 53
four 153
fourth 143
fox 81
friend 100
frog 104
from 26
front 68
full 54
funny 11

game 42
games 103
gaped 134
gapped 134
gas 82
gave 67
genie 111
genies 113
get 23
getting 23
ghost 102
gift 75
girl 19
girls 5
giving 80

glad 49
glass 119
glasses 39
go 63
goes 35
going 5
gold 29
gone 143
good 20
got 81
grabbed 28
grape 150
grass 49
grasshop-
per 145
green 104
grew 99
ground 51
grow 64
grown 100

hadn't 149
hair 126
hall 31
handed 83
handle 152
handsome 132
hanging 52
happen 64
happened 64
happening 140
happy 10
hard 21
hardest 126
has 3
hasn't 149
hat 66
hatched 99
hate 66
hated 153
hater 116
hates 22
hatter 116
have 92
haven't 117
having 85
he 4

head 39
heap 103
hear 22
hears 117
heave 85
heaved 108
heel 113
held 27
hello 100
help 10
helped 10
helper 96
helps 131
hens 142
her 3
here 3
here's 160
herself 51
he'll 108
he's 123
hey 160
hid 56
hide 56
himself 41
hitting 84
hold 26
holding 57
hole 6
holes 83
home 68
homes 102
honey 130
hop 44
hope 35
hoped 94
hoping 97
hopped 84
hopper 109
hopping 96
horn 26
horse 12
horses 103
hotter 133
hound 50
hounds 52
house 48
how 48

howling 105
hug 123
hugged 61
human 121
hundred 67
hung 127
hungry 123
hunter 141
hunting 67

ice 80
icebox 114
idea 157
if 94
impossible 121
insect 142
inside 36
instant 123
into 56
it's 121
I'll 34
I'm 55
I've 75

jail 91
jailer 91
Jan 130
Jane 17
Japan 126
Jean 146
jerk 141
Jill 19
job 77
joke 134
jumped 15
jumping 17
jumps 28
jungle 141
junk 114
just 45

keep 58
kept 30
key 90
kick 43
kicked 40
kill 142

kind 21
king 102
kissed 2
kit 60
kite 60
kites 62
kitten 101
kittens 102
knew 139
knock 107
knocked 108
know 63
knows 124

lady 30
lake 57
landed 63
large 158
last 34
later 145
laugh 102
laughed 106
laughing 104
lay 132
lead 107
leaf 106
leaned 140
leaning 143
leap 99
leave 23
leaves 94
leaving 75
led 24
left 33
legs 26
let 93
letter 159
let's 15
lick 34
licked 160
licking 160
lie 55
lied 72
lies 114
life 125
lift 1
lifted 63

light 136
like 10
liked 7
likes 20
lined 139
lion 141
lions 138
listen 137
live 5
lived 6
load 71
loaded 130
loading 74
long 87
longer 87
longest 150
look 23
looked 11
looking 37
looks 12
loop 158
loud 45
loudly 140
love 28
loved 41
lucky 95
lunch 101
lying 74

mad 48
made 7
magic 51
mail 2
main 31
make 65
maker 64
makes 64
making 64
mall 34
mammal 149
many 54
mark 74
Marta
Flores 121
master 111
masters 125
mate 127

matter 146
maybe 111
meal 23
mean 74
meaner 107
meanest 105
meat 67
meets 35
melt 114
men 86
mess 84
metal 155
mice 132
middle 115
might 110
mile 139
miles 31
milk 102
mind 157
minute 127
missing 68
mixed 77
mole 34
money 27
monkey 155
monster 104
moo 48
mooing 49
moon 24
mop 82
mope 81
moped 89
moping 88
mopped 82
mopper 82
mopping 83
more 29
morning 159
most 89
mother 20
motor 160
mountain 50
mouse 48
mouth 80
move 126
moves 130
Mr. 139

much 37
muddy 152
must 25
my 24
myself 106

nail 133
nailed 89
name 19
named 19
names 100
nap 160
near 74
nearly 143
need 89
needed 45
needs 101
nest 101
never 7
new 101
next 15
nice 132
night 103
nine 68
ninety 69
no 63
nobody 87
none 100
not 42
note 24
noted 92
notes 91
nothing 86
now 91
number 129

oak 91
obey 124
of 3
off 29
oh 35
okay 72
old 26
once 50
one 30
only 52
open 52

opened 53
or 66
other 10
Ott 112
ouch 52
our 48
out 45
outside 70
over 16
owl 139

packed 90
packing 127
pad 24
page 148
pain 141
paint 2
painted 26
painting 25
pals 100
pan 57
pane 57
panes 110
pans 110
pants 29
paper 62
park 60
parked 69
part 37
parting 120
parts 76
party 35
passed 78
passing 130
past 45
path 139
paths 149
patted 125
paw 141
pay 23
peach 113
peaches 113
peek 111
peevish 145
people 102
pepper 139
person 121

petted 48
phone 126
phoned 128
pick 46
picked 35
pile 67
piled 50
piles 39
pin 59
pine 59
pined 90
pink 29
pinned 90
place 125
plan 81
plane 66
planed 120
planer 121
planing 123
planned 120
planner 121
planning 104
plant 90
planted 92
planting 93
plants 90
plate 108
play 20
played 10
player 43
playing 33
plays 12
please 36
plop 108
pocket 130
pond 133
poof 116
poorest 116
popped 148
pouch 50
pow 84
pretty 64
prince 144
proud 64
puff 112
pull 141
pulled 136

puppy 160
push 160
put 39

question 98
quick 157
quickly 159
quiet 157
quietly 158

rabbit 20
race 138
raft 143
rail 66
rammed 108
rang 127
rat 51
rate 51
rather 155
reach 101
reached 55
read 20
reading 20
ready 43
real 17
really 20
red 152
remember 115
remembering 149
rent 128
rental 128
rented 129
rest 52
resting 118
rich 56
richest 121
rid 152
ride 14
rides 20
right 92
ring 125
rip 31
road 1
roared 105
rob 27
robbed 105
robber 60

robbers 27	sea 143	silly 36	snow 78	stay 14
robed 105	seat 96	simple 122	soaked 66	stayed 57
rocky 149	seed 90	sing 36	soft 151	stays 105
rod 40	seem 71	singing 132	sold 29	steal 60
rode 15	seems 91	sinking 143	some 16	steep 51
rolled 111	self 20	sip 110	somebody 81	steer 157
rolling 35	selling 30	sister 19	someday 138	steering 158
Rome 115	send 90	sit 55	someone 65	step 114
room 24	sent 90	site 55	something 56	stepped 136
roots 135	service 129	sitting 1	sometimes 103	steps 25
rope 17	sets 70	six 28	soon 19	stick 119
round 56	setting 55	sixteen 147	sore 26	sticks 90
rubbed 56	shade 120	skates 130	sorry 72	still 24
rubs 112	shake 63	sky 28	sound 51	stones 97
rule 146	shaking 63	slammed 52	sounded 115	stood 121
rules 151	shares 144	sleek 158	sounds 49	stool 135
runner 44	shark 10	sleep 35	space 146	stop 5
running 60	sharks 12	sleepy 150	spank 119	stopped 14
rush 126	sharp 61	slept 145	spanking 115	store 27
rushed 127	she 3	slid 133	speak 144	storm 111
	shed 70	slide 134	speed 140	story 19
sadder 65	sheep 102	slider 132	spell 95	strange 112
safe 138	shell 134	sliding 135	spelled 127	stream 15
said 86	she'd 123	slipped 79	spelling 128	streaming 117
salad 142	she'll 158	slop 92	spells 108	street 23
salt 34	she's 74	slope 92	spend 125	string 62
Sam 65	shine 133	slowest 139	spent 94	striped 151
same 16	shining 133	slowly 53	spider 141	stripes 153
Sandy 68	shirt 145	sly 80	spin 116	strong 135
sang 132	shoe 145	small 33	spitting 122	strongest 141
save 61	shoes 146	smart 95	splash 15	stuck 79
saved 49	shook 66	smarter 124	splat 118	stuff 127
saves 144	shoot 82	smartest 124	spot 22	such 132
saw 34	shop 74	smash 114	spotted 34	sucked 144
say 82	shopping 104	smelled 22	spring 157	suddenly 113
saying 82	shore 111	smile 59	squeak 159	super 81
says 73	short 125	smiled 37	stairs 82	swam 11
scare 66	shot 45	smiles 84	stall 34	swan 100
scared 72	should 37	smiling 110	stand 36	sweet 138
school 67	shouldn't 42	smoke 112	standing 68	swell 128
schools 95	shout 45	snake 110	star 46	swim 10
score 41	shouted 49	snap 135	stare 121	swimming 11
scored 42	show 79	snapped 124	stared 158	swims 12
scores 43	showed 75	sneak 135	start 6	swing 92
scream 109	shy 110	sneaking 147	started 16	swinging 147
screamed 50	Sid 69	sneaky 136	starting 7	swung 93
screaming 143	side 23	sniffed 144	starts 62	

table 40
tail 160
take 58
taken 126
takes 113
taking 124
talk 5
talked 82
talking 5
tall 34
taller 37
tallest 150
tame 96
tap 83
tape 84
taped 88
taper 158
tapped 83
tapper 158
tapping 94
tar 73
tart 7
teacher 48
teaches 94
team 42
tear 87
tears 134
teeth 129
telling 108
tent 77
test 113
than 28
thank 38
thanked 88
that 1
that's 73
the 1
their 74
them 3
themselves 107
then 1
there 2
these 4
they 4
they'll 156
they've 126
thick 140

thing 78
things 17
think 29
thinking 37
third 151
this 1
thorn 141
those 4
thousand 53
thousands 115
three 30
threw 144
through 118
throw 86
thud 121
thumb 144
thunder 64
tickle 105
tickled 149
tiger 96
Tim 64
time 45
timer 160
times 83
tired 55
title 100
toad 105
today 65
toe 133
told 25
tone 96
tonight 146
too 127
took 11
toot 27
tooth 135
torn 141
tossed 92
touch 14
touched 53
touching 38
town 158
tracks 68
train 67
trained 126
tramp's 145
trapped 65

trapper 154
treat 127
trick 81
tricks 103
tried 19
tries 150
trip 30
trips 129
trouble 129
truck 71
true 122
trunk 128
try 14
trying 14
turn 105
turned 104
turns 127
turtle 131
tv 66
two 64

ugly 100
understand 127
until 128
used 136
using 150
U.S. 158

van 126
vane 126
vaned 127
very 4
vine 150
vow 124
vows 125

wade 66
wading 66
wagged 96
wait 97
waited 71
waiting 139
walk 5
walked 24
walking 5
wall 45
walls 85

Walter 41
Walter's 43
want 28
wanted 30
wants 46
warm 155
warmer 157
watch 137
watched 104
watching 138
water 17
waved 115
waving 144
we 110
wear 133
weed 134
week 38
well 23
went 1
were 4
west 127
wet 101
we'll 62
we're 117
we've 123
whale 156
what 16
what's 74
wheels 157
when 2
whenever 143
where 2
where's 129
which 99
while 65
white 25
who 25
why 3
wide 131
wig 99
will 22
win 38
wind 62
window 79
windows 119
wings 132
winter 156

wiped 125
wise 118
wish 154
wished 117
wishes 111
wishing 73
with 10
wizard 145
woke 55
wolf 137
wolves 137
woman 67
wonder 152
wonderful 120
won't 63
wood 62
wooden 150
woods 81
woof 159
word 39
words 90
work 58
worked 77
worker 138
works 107
world 133
would 36
wouldn't 41

yard 4
yarn 6
year 111
years 17
yelled 11
yelling 93
yellow 30
yes 7
yet 120
you 88
your 38
yourself 125
you'll 62
you're 98
you've 126

Individual Fluency Checkout Chart

Name	5	10	15	20	25	30	35	40	45	50	55	60	65	70	75	80	85	90	95	100	105	110	115	120	125	130	135	140	145	150	155	160

SCOPE AND SEQUENCE CHART

SOUNDS AND LETTER NAMES

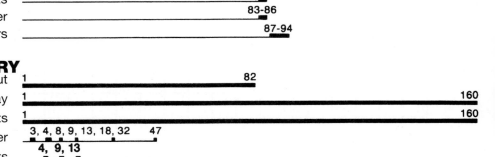

Sounds	1 — 39	
Sound Combinations (Diphthongs and Digraphs)	1 — 160	
Letter Names—Vowels	40 52	
Letter Names—Consonants	83-86	
Alphabetical Order	83-86	
Capital Letters	87-94	

READING VOCABULARY

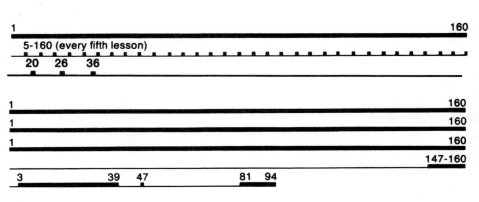

Sound Out	1 — 82	
Read the Fast Way	1 — 160	
Word Parts	1 — 160	
Hard Words in Reader	3, 4, 8, 9, 13, 18, 32 — 47	
*Hard Words in Reader Tests	4, 9, 13	
Final-e Rule	48 — 80	
Spell by Letter Names	86 — 160	

STORIES

Decoding

Oral Story Reading	1 — 160	
*Fluency: Rate/Accuracy Checkouts	5-160 (every fifth lesson)	
*Group Accuracy Tests	20 26 36	

Comprehension

Story	1 — 160	
Comprehension—Oral	1 — 160	
Story Comprehension—Written	1 — 160	
Picture Comprehension	1 — 160	
Rule Review	147-160	
Read the Items	3 — 39 47 — 81 94	

INDEPENDENT WORKSHEET EXERCISES

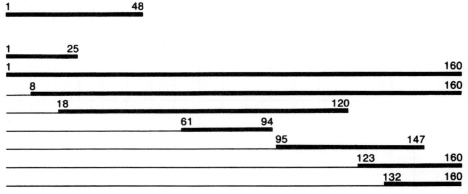

Mechanics

Sounds and Sentence Copying	1 — 48	

Comprehension

Picture Comprehension	1 — 25	
Story Items	1 — 160	
Reading Comprehension Passages	8 — 160	
Following Instructions	18 — 120	
Story-Picture Items	61 — 94	
Picture Deductions	95 — 147	
Written Deductions	123 — 160	
Factual Information Passages	132 — 160	

LESSON 11

Note: Children who are placed at lesson 11 in the reading program begin at lesson 11 in the spelling program.

SOUND WRITING
EXERCISE 1

Write **a, h, i, s, e**

a. You're going to write some sounds.
b. Here's the first sound you're going to write. Listen. **aaa.** What sound? (Signal.) *aaa.*
c. Write **aaa.** ✔
d. Next sound.
   Listen. **h.** What sound? (Signal.) *h.*
e. Write **h.** ✔
f. (Repeat steps *d* and *e* for **i, s,** and **e.**)

EXERCISE 2

Introduce sound combination **th**

a. (Write on the board: **th.**)
b. (Point to **th.**) Everybody, tell me the sound these letters make. Get ready. (Signal.) *th.* Yes, **th.**
c. (Erase **th.**) Everybody, write the letters that go together and make the sound **th.** ✔

WORD WRITING
EXERCISE 3

Read, say the sounds, write **sit, rat**

a. (Write **sit** on the board.)
b. Everybody, read this word the fast way. Get ready.
   (Signal.) *Sit.*
• What word? (Signal.) *Sit.* Yes, **sit.**
c. My turn to say the sounds in **sit** the hard way. (Touch each sound.) **sss** (pause) **iii** (pause) **t.**
d. Your turn. Say the sounds in **sit** the hard way. Get ready. (Touch each sound as children say:) *sss* (pause) *iii* (pause) *t.*

e. (Erase **sit.**) I'll tap for each sound. You say the sounds in **sit** the hard way. Get ready. (Tap for each sound as children say:) *sss* (pause) *iii* (pause) *t.*
• (Repeat until firm.)
f. Everybody, write the word (pause) **sit.**
g. (Repeat steps *a–f* for **rat.**)

EXERCISE 4

Read, say the sounds, write **man, fit, he**

a. (Write **man** on the board.)
b. Everybody, read this word the fast way. Get ready. (Signal.) *Man.*
• What word? (Signal.) *Man.* Yes, **man.**
c. Say the sounds in **man** the hard way. (Touch each sound as the children say:) *mmm* (pause) *aaa* (pause) *nnn.*
d. (Erase **man.**) I'll tap for each sound. You say the sounds in **man** the hard way. Get ready. (Tap for each sound as the children say:) *mmm* (pause) *aaa* (pause) *nnn.*
• (Repeat until firm.)
e. Everybody, write the word (pause) **man.** ✔
f. (Repeat steps *a–e* for **fit** and **he.**)

LESSON 105

EXERCISE 1
WORD COMPLETION

a. (Write on the board:)

> 1. _ _ op
> 2. _ all
> 3. sa _ t
> 4. f _ _ m

b. Copy the board. ✔
c. One or more letters are missing from these words. You're going to write the missing letters.
d. Word 1 is supposed to be **shop.**
• What word? (Signal.) *Shop.*
• Fill in the blanks so that the word spells **shop.**
e. Word 2 is supposed to be **mall.**
• What word? (Signal.) *Mall.*
• Fill in the blanks so that the word spells **mall.**
f. (Repeat step *d* for **3. salt, 4. farm.**)
g. Get ready to spell the words you just wrote.
h. Look at word 1.
• What word? (Signal.) *Shop.*
• Spell **shop.** Get ready. (Signal.) *S-H-O-P.*
• Fix it if it's not spelled right.
i. (Repeat step *h* for **2. mall, 3. salt, 4. farm.**)

EXERCISE 2
SPELLING WORDS

a. (Write on the board:)

> 1. was
> 2. what
> 3. march
> 4. fall

b. Word 1 is **was.** Spell **was.** Get ready. (Signal.) *W-A-S.*
c. Word 2 is **what.** Spell **what.** Get ready. (Signal.) *W-H-A-T.*
d. (Repeat step *c* for **3. march, 4. fall.**)
• (Erase the board.)
e. Spell those words without looking.
f. Word 1 is **was.** Spell **was.** Get ready. (Signal.) *W-A-S.*
g. Word 2 is **what.** Spell **what.** Get ready. (Signal.) *W-H-A-T.*
h. (Repeat step *g* for **3. march, 4. fall.**)

EXERCISE 3
SPELLING REVIEW

a. Get ready to spell and write some words.
b. Word 1 is **we.** What word? (Signal.) *We.* Spell **we.** Get ready. (Signal.) *W-E.*
• Write it. ✔
c. Word 2 is **where.** What word? (Signal.) *Where.*
• Spell **where.** Get ready. (Signal.) *W-H-E-R-E.*
• Write it. ✔
d. (Repeat step *c* for **3. are, 4. do.**)
e. I'll spell each word.
• Put an **X** next to any word you missed and write that word correctly.
• (Spell each word twice. Write the words on the board as you spell them.)